VOICE OF THE FISH

VOICE OF THE FISH

A Lyric Essay

Lars Horn

Graywolf Press

This publication is made possible, in part, by the voters of Minnesota through a Minnesota State Arts Board Operating Support grant, thanks to a legislative appropriation from the arts and cultural heritage fund. Significant support has also been provided by the National Endowment for the Arts, the McKnight Foundation, the Lannan Foundation, the Amazon Literary Partnership, and other generous contributions from foundations, corporations, and individuals. To these organizations and individuals we offer our heartfelt thanks.

Published by Graywolf Press
212 Third Avenue North, Suite 485
Minneapolis, Minnesota 55401

This is a work of nonfiction. It is also a work of memory and craft. On occasion, names, places, and events have been altered in the interest of personal privacy and artistic intent.

www.graywolfpress.org

Published in the United States of America

ISBN 978-1-64445-089-5 (paperback)
ISBN 978-1-64445-177-9 (ebook)

2 4 6 8 9 7 5 3 1
First Graywolf Printing, 2022

Library of Congress Control Number: 2021945923

Cover design: Kapo Ng

Cover art: Shutterstock

For my mother and father,
Sheridan Horn and David Horn

For my wife, Jaquira Díaz

I mean *river* as a verb. A happening. It is moving within me right now.

~

This is not juxtaposition. Body and water are not *two unlike things*—
they are more than *close together or side by side.* They are *same*—body,
being, energy, prayer, current, motion, medicine.

The body is beyond six senses. Is sensual. An ecstatic state of energy,
always on the verge of praying, or entering any river of movement.

Energy is a moving river moving my moving body.

—Natalie Diaz, "The First Water Is the Body"

Contents

On June 23, 1626, a fishmonger of Cambridge market discovered a century-old manuscript in the belly of a codfish. Half-dissolved and wrapped in sailcloth, the sextodecimo fell into the hands of Dr. Mede of Christ's College, Cambridge, who happened to be walking through the market that day. *Vox piscis* or *The Book-Fish*, as the manuscript became known, was published a year later and contained several theological treatises: *The preparation to the Crosse and to death*; *A mirrour, or, glasse, to know thy selfe*; *A briefe instruction, to teach a person willingly to die, and not to feare death*; *The treasure of knowledge*.

The texts were attributed to the Protestant reformer John Frith, who, during his lifetime, spent months imprisoned in the belly of an Oxford fish cellar on charges of heresy. Sentenced to death on June 23, 1533, Frith was burnt at the stake in Smithfield, London—upwards of 250 nautical miles from King's Lynn, where the codfish was finally landed ninety-three years later.

VOICE OF THE FISH

In Water Disjointed from Me

In childhood photographs, I blur within a bath of dead squid, sleep atop hot concrete, severed magpie wings splayed across my back. My mother always distrusted conventional family portraits and, along with mirrors and weighing scales, banned them from the house. The body was movement, volume, was rhythm through space. The body was not to be looked at. Except when that looking made it strange. When the stilling of a body undid it. Lent an enduring instability.

I experience my body as interiority that radiates. Mirrors unnerve me. I don't know my weight. I don't tend to look at myself. I like gestures. Words come least naturally to me—I tend to think in images, textures.

In the summer of 2014, I tore the muscles from my right shoulder to my lower back while weightlifting. After two months, the injury hadn't healed. Not even begun to. As it turned out, I would spend the next six months bedbound, medicated, unable to wash or dress myself. Doctors would fail to explain the lack of progress, and I, having exhausted the list of hospital units, would return to bed, watch flickering images on an old television set. Around the same time, I lost the ability to speak, read, or write. At first, I stuttered; later, I remained silent. As for reading, I could manage a line, but any more and I felt nauseous. I still can't fully explain this loss of language, why my body caved—exhaustion, depression, the sheer physical pain. But living for six months in a body that wouldn't adhere to words, that balked at sentences, made me aware of the body as texture. As image and gesture. Rhythm. As varying weight.

After those months of illness, I wanted to write differently, wanted language and narrative to carry more physicality. Come as the thud of soil burying a face. Plummet—a bird petrifying as it enters a lake. To adhere to a visual or gestural logic. Less "worded," more photographic. More movement.

I quit academia, research, a translation career. I started over.

I have always found pronouns to be slippery, distant things. At school, I wrote and talked about myself in the third person masculine. My teacher expressed concern. My mother, thank Christ, replied: "So, the kid's fucking weird. They all are. Give it time."

I remember the evening my mother knelt down, sighed: "Lars, my love, you've got to start writing 'I' for homework." I stood there—crew cut, boys' clothing, boys' toys, a boys' bike. And my mother in front of me—men's shirt, men's boots, a woman who, in her own words, *was never meant to be a mother, because she was queer.* A woman who decided not to abort when she fell pregnant by the man she was about to divorce for a woman; who, when she phoned the UK Lesbian and Gay Helpline in 1988, was told that if she mentioned her sexuality as a motive for divorce, she would lose child custody, her teaching job, would remain unemployable. This woman, who has lived in the closet her whole life, from family, friends—from me until I was eleven—she looked at me, not saying anything, both of us just looking at one another. Even then, I didn't like the direction in which this was going.

I came home that week with a writing assignment: *What I Did This Weekend*. I remember how the sentences clotted, disintegrated every time I thought them. How I broke them before they hit paper: *He buried a cat.—I, I buried a cat.*

I learnt to use this "I"—to speak and write and do as if my body somehow reverberated within this sound. But I have never felt comfortable with an "I," or in bringing any concept of "me" as a self to language. I find silence and physicality come more naturally. And distance. To feel oneself as "over there," as nebulous. Within and without.

Nonbinary, transmasculine—my gender exists, for the most part, as unseen, unworded, unintelligible. It is instead reduced to the gender I was assigned at birth, as if any counter to this will always be less "real." Somehow, gender requires corporeal inscription to be accepted. I regularly find myself trying to explain my gender in terms that will make it intelligible to another. Yet despite trying to explain how pronouns still carry somewhere in water disjointed from me. How I sense myself as movement. As lake or late-night radio. As a thing that feels weighted, finds it hard to rise, break surface. Eventually, these attempts return crudely to bodily specifics, usually of erogenous zones.

What might gender look like written beyond the blurring of a male-female binary? The body expanded beyond its periphery—animal, vegetable, mineral. Textural. Gestural. The body—hard and soft, a thing to be warmed or cooled, wrapped in cloth.

During the months I was ill, I kept trying to read: a new book, a short book, chapter, story, a poem, books that I'd read before, books whose openings I knew by heart—all this accompanied by exhaustion, vertigo, nausea. I would lie still after that. Numb. The body drawing blank after blank, static thoughts greying over bedsheets.

I remember the first book I read about a year later. I read it slowly, a paragraph at a time. It was Oscar Moore's *PWA*. A collection of Moore's newspaper columns written as he was living with AIDS. Everything about that book lifted this body. Its gentleness, its humour. Its generosity.

Since falling ill, I believe writing to be a vital act. All the more so when it comes from bodies so often marginalised or written over. I look to writing—urgent, unusual writing—as an art that can make someone feel seen, feel relevant. For a moment, writing can prove wide enough for another to stand within. Breathe out.

Literature alters the texture of things—how we are, or do, or see. I write with the hope that, for someone somewhere, these words might prove a salve. Might rinse the eyes, warm the chest. Ultimately, though, I hope these words might bring someone, whoever they are, back to themself—differently.

Last Night, a Pike Swam up the Stairs

I.   Perch circled the skirting boards.
Sticklebacks twitched at the foot of the bed.

II. As a child, I believed my body thrummed with fishes. I drew pictures: the body aqueous—ovular, amorphous—walled by cartilage, algae, silt. Eels coiled in the stomach. Anemones pulsed in the gut. And always a pike—lone, muscular—writhed up the throat.

III. When I matured physically and my body began not to fit, I always wondered whether it had nothing to do with biology or hormones. Whether it was because the fishes had stayed or left.

IV.   "There is also the pike. These, as Aristotle reports, are a solitary and carnivorous fish; and they have a bony tongue, adhering to the mouth, and a triangular heart. . . . In shrewdness he is superior to other fish, being very ingenious at devising means to save himself; on which account, Aristophanes the comic poet says—

"The pike, the wisest of all fish that swim.

"And . . . Archestratus says—

"Take the large cestris cephalus from Gæson,
When you do come to fair Miletus' city.
Take too the pike, the offspring of the gods."
    —Athenaeus of Naucratis, *The Deipnosophists, or Banquet of the Learned of Athenaeus*

V.   To be captivated by violence—pulsing blue light. To stand transfixed, face pressed to eight-inch acrylic. My mother gave me her love of water, of scaled, fronded life. My mother gave me her strange love of aquariums—an attraction, a repulsion. The same fraught interest that led her to photograph me again and again before fish tanks, my body growing, morphing to the slip of manta rays, ribbon eels, sharks. All of us captured, spectator and spectacle shimmering across the glass. Their bodies long dead by now, mine still shifting, propelling slowly through the days, sloughing itself. But, momentarily, all of us—caught in light and gelatin, still together as we fade from chromogenic paper.

VI.   In one series taken with a timer, I glance at a penguin cresting towards me in the tank. Three shots:

the penguin ever better in view, and me—four years old, ever more twisted, the camera lens abandoned, looking only at the penguin. Only wanting that: to look, not to be looked at.

VII.   Florida, USA, 1996: Docks. A tugboat—sky blue, sponges strung between cabin and mast. Heat banding off the boardwalk, the water, off pelicans' outstretched wings. My mother hurried me to a nearby building. Once used to store engines and nets, the hangar had been swept clean. Hand-painted signs littered the entrance: *SHARK FISHING, FULL DAY EXCURSION—CATCH GUARANTEED!* Shade swelled over my feet. I walked forward, blinked. An air pump whirred. My mother removed her sunglasses: "There, look at that." A cylindrical tank towered in the midst of the darkness. I stepped closer, my skin humming aquamarine. A sand tiger shark circled the glass. Its shadow glided over my mother's eyes, lips, neck. My mother picked up her Nikon, lifted me onto the tank ledge: "Face me, Lars. That's it. Now wait. I missed it. Stay there. Keep looking at the camera. No, ignore that. It doesn't matter what they think. Wait. It's too dark. Okay, hold still, the shark's coming back." The searing white of a camera flash—once, twice, three times. On our way out, I overheard a staff member say, "I don't know what's gotten into him. He leapt in the tank and ate Bobby, a few of the smaller fish too."
       "Leapt?"
       "Clean leapt out and back down into the tank."
       I read the sign: *NO FLASH!*

VIII.   In the photograph, I wear navy shorts, my chest is bare, my hair midlength, sun-bleached. I glow. Bluish-green.

Androgynous. A body that hesitates: male, female, something else, something more, perhaps. Inches behind me, the sand tiger shark skims the wall of the tank—snout, gills, dorsal and caudal fins—seven feet and two hundred pounds of muscle, fat, of sandpaper skin.

IX.   I remember that childhood holiday to Florida as a rush of heat and colour, as skittering geckos and soaring pelicans. It is strange to think of myself then, a child caught in the neon and fiberglass of Florida's tourist docks, spray exploding over the boardwalk. To think of myself caught in the sticky heat, palms chittering, in a place more vivid than anywhere I'd ever been. I couldn't know that I'd return decades later. That I'd live there, drive hot metal through grinding traffic, egrets fluttering through sirens, shouts. That, some twenty years after our holiday in Florida, after I'd grown, attended universities, acquired and lost jobs, made and lost friends, this photo of me and the shark would resurface—fall from the pages of a book. My mother would text me a copy. And this image— photograph of a photograph, colours filmy—would find its way back to me, slap up through the years like bleached plastic, brine-streaked and tangled in kelp.

X.   Written in the third century AD, Athenaeus of Naucratis's *The Deipnosophists* or *Dinner-Table Philosophers* is a fifteen-volume work of fictional banquet conversations supposedly held between esteemed philosophers, physicians, grammarians, lexicographers, jurists, and musicians—themselves either fictional or long dead. The work references some 700 earlier Greek writers and 2,500 texts. Considered the world's oldest cookbook, whilst also renowned for its clear portrait of homosexuality in late Hellenism, the book's subject matter ranges from "Lentils" to "Spare Livers," from the "Use of Silver Plate" to the "Misconduct of Fishermen." And in this same work—indeed, where else?—one finds mention of a ship built by Archimedes for the tyrant Hiero II, a ship of gargantuan proportions whose floors depicted the *Iliad* in mosaic, whose hull held a gymnasium, variegated marble baths, gardens, horses, and, crucially, a fish well of vast proportion.

XI.   "There was also a cistern near the head of the ship, carefully shut, and containing two thousand measures of water, made of beams closely compacted with pitch and canvass. And next to the cistern there was a large Water-tight well for fish, made so with beams of wood and lead. And it was kept full of sea-water, and great numbers of fish were kept in it."

          —Athenaeus of Naucratis, *The Deipnosophists, or*
          Banquet of the Learned of Athenaeus

XII.   For almost two millennia, this early form of fish tank seemed as mythic as Hiero II's watercraft. But, between 1958 and 1959, construction workers excavating grounds for the Leonardo da Vinci airport in Fiumicino, Italy, unearthed the remains of several ancient vessels. Far from the planes expected to roar over that land—snarls of metal, petrol, and plastic hurtling above the earth—the workers found crafts fated not to air but to water. Discovered on the former site of a harbour basin—a building project undertaken by Emperor Claudius in AD 42—entire hulls of Roman cargo ships groaned from the sludge. Ships that would once have carried 7,500 sacks of grain, some 3,000 jars of wine or oil. One set of ruins stood out. Referred to as "Fiumicino 5," they belonged to a fishing boat complete with *navis vivaria* or "live tank." Constructed from wooden planks coated in lead, the tank would have held seawater and live fish, thus facilitating the transportation of catch to market. Confirmer of myth recovered by accident, the ancient tank is the sole example in existence from Roman times.

XIII.   When the photograph of myself in Florida made its way back to me, I couldn't help but look at it. I made it the background on my phone. Eating alone at a roadside diner, I pressed the home button, looked again for the brief seconds of a timed bulb: a shark and a seven-year-old flared into darkness, surfaced from a waterlogged night.

XIV.   This photograph is more complicated than those where I am three or four. My expression—not quite fear, more wariness, distrust. As if, somehow, in just seven years of living, I realised I wasn't quite what this world wanted. At least, not what people wanted; animals, plants—they didn't care. My mother also didn't give a damn. She let me wear boys' underwear, boys' clothes, play with boys' toys. She never curtailed how I navigated this body or its place in the world. But I did not fit. And, on some level, I seemed aware of it. TV, books, films—no one else came jarring in their own skin. At school, none of the girls swam in trunks, threw off their T-shirt in hot weather to play football. No one blunted towards different limbs.

XV.   I became increasingly uneasy in photographs. At fifteen, I shrank from cameras. Even in those few years between three and seven, my relationship to the world altered. After weeks of staring at the photograph of myself with the shark, I realised it was here, in eyes lit with electricity, here, at seven years old, that I already knew the danger of being seen, that my own body could be mobilised against me.

XVI.   Looking at this photograph on the bus, in launderettes, in quiet drifts of empty time, I wondered if I might be able to write of my oldest obsessions: water, aquatic life. If I might let them glide, softly sweep and tide—an undercurrent to clear moments, to images hurled upwards, foaming across rocks. To feel at disjoint from one's body. To not recognise it as one's own. The photograph of myself at seven pulsed this book alive. Propelled me to write of the gulf between myself and my body—strange chasm that still snakes with life.

XVII.   "In several country seats . . . fish eat out of the hand, but . . . at Helorus, a fortress of Sicily not far from Syracuse, and likewise in the spring of Jupiter of Labraynda, the eels even wear ear-rings."
                              —Pliny the Elder, *Naturalis historia*

XVIII.   A religious shrine and pilgrimage site for the Karians, Labraynda sits on a mountainside overlooking modern-day Milas. A natural spring rushes from beneath a rock seemingly cleft in two by a lightning bolt—the shrine's focal point and reason for being singled out as a place of worship.

XIX.   In the 1940s, Swedish archaeologists excavated Labraynda. They unearthed a temple to Zeus, three andirons or male club buildings, two stoas, two

Roman baths, priests' lodgings, a nymphaeum, a stadium, and a potential treasury—all enclosed, at the
site's periphery, by tombs and sepulchres. Set apart
from the banqueting halls and lodgings, archaeologists discovered what appears to be the fountain and
pool of Pliny the Elder's bejewelled eels. Adorned
with gold earrings and necklaces, these fish were kept
as oracular aids and used to decipher messages from
the gods. And, so, as animals of hoof and hide were
sacrificed at the annual five-day feast to Zeus, their
bones and fat burnt as offerings; as men wrestled
and ran in the stadium, pitting earthbound flesh
against earthbound flesh; as servants butchered and
cooked carcasses for the feast, the eels, just paces
from this thick pulse of blood and fat and fur and
mud, of gulped fetid air, the eels circled—untouched,
uninterrupted—their watery world so much closer to
the ether of the gods.

XX. Even centuries later, as the Swedish archaeologists
examined the far reaches of the site, one location remained unobtainable: the spring. The site's origin
point and likely location of its oldest artefacts, the
spring proved impossible to excavate. Each time archaeologists dug around it, water rose up through the
soil, rushed, flooded the trenches. I sometimes wonder whether the archaeologists ever saw the water
whorl, the mud writhe, whether the land ever moved
once more with glistening muscular life.

XXI. "Men tell of the moray belonging to Crassus the Roman,
which had been adorned with earrings and small necklaces set with jewels, just like some lovely maiden; and
when Crassus called it, it would recognise his voice and

come swimming up, and whatever he offered it, it would
eagerly and promptly take and eat. Now when this fish
died Crassus, so I am told, actually mourned for it and
buried it. And on one occasion when Domitius said to
him 'You fool, mourning for a dead moray!' Crassus
took him up with these words: 'I mourned for a moray,
but you never mourned for the three wives you buried.'"
—Claudius Aelian, *On the Nature of Animals*

XXII.   RECURRING DREAM:

My body, sternum sawn in two.
Chest clamps, green linen, anemones—red, purple,
ringed deep blue.
A chest of soft membranes—squirming, shining—
recoils from the hum of strip lights.
A surgeon transfers the anemones to a steel dish.
That they not disturb the pike.
That they close my body.
That the light breaks, the room plunged beneath
water—rush of a knifefish. Shock, white voltage.
That I sink, body into bull kelp, mud, into tides.
That my body tide.

XXIII.   As a child, I made lists of fishes. All kinds of lists:
weights, speeds, historical facts. Some of those lists
enumerated species that change sex as a matter of
course:

Maturing into an adult male, the ribbon eel takes on a
bluish tint. But, when an adult male ribbon eel reaches
full size, it changes gender, turning from blue-black to
searing yellow.

Noting these aquatic bodies helped dissolve a world
I found too hard, too strict in how it required me to

live within it. These lists were never about me equating being trans to being less human. They were more an attempt to denaturalise the ways humans have bound up the parameters of our own species: the "normal," the "natural," the "scientifically justifiable," the "real." Being human has been, and always will be, filtered through essentialisms, dogma, ideologies, will always be caught between humanity's capacity to love and hate.

XXIV. CLOWN FISH: *Born male, all clown fish live and die within a single gender, all except the most dominant male, who, reaching this position in the shoal, transitions to female.*

XXV. It is a privilege of power and normativity—white, cisgender, heterosexual, able-bodied—to proclaim oneself an animal. Scientifically speaking, we are exactly that, but its declaration toes a dangerous line, science having so often reserved the animalistic for those who fall outside of a society's dominant ideologies. Slavery, segregation, genocide, slow dismembering by law and court: humanity and animality have always existed along fraught, fragile lines.

XXVI. The majority's humanity is never in doubt. And yet: "the majority"—slipperiest body of all. A gamble, on rank oil.

XXVII. PARROTFISH: *Highest in the social order of parrotfish is the adult "super-male," a role fulfilled solely by the most dominant female of a mating group. Following the death of a "super-male," the dominant female changes sex, the parrotfish now larger, markedly more vibrant than typical males.*

XXVIII.   My body a mass of fishes—to dredge these truths from my lungs, watch them contort in someone else's mouth. I simply relented, plunged them back down. For years, I never wrote of my ease around water, of seeing myself, night after night: my body caught in a dark tide, rippling—caudal, dorsal, clouding sand, fronded kelp. I couldn't find a way to honestly render this body—my experience or understanding of it—the fins, the gills, muzzle, hide. And yet, seeing how regularly sex cannot be reduced to a simple binary in other species—more rite of passage than destination, a threshold through which one may flicker back and fore—I feel so much *more* human. As if it were proof, reassurance from some disappeared god. As if Neptune roused himself, sent shimmering answer from lightless depth.

XXIX.   *TURRITOPSIS DOHRNII: In the face of starvation, physical threat, or bodily impairment, the* Turritopsis dohrnii *species of jellyfish can revert to an embryonic state and reproduce asexually. During this process, the jellyfish's cells transform entirely: muscle becomes nerve or sperm or egg; biological time reverses; and as for the body— supposedly singular thing—it shatters, multiplying.*

XXX.   When did the gods retire? Zeus, Hades, Neptune— where did they dive to no longer hear the growling earth?

XXXI.   I find solace in the world, in water and aquatic bodies—clams, Greenland sharks, bowheaded whales, sponges—lifespans of centuries, sometimes millennia. What must they witness during their slow pulse through the world? These entities that endure through innumerable lives. That guard, balance, keep rhythm amidst this frenetic slur of human life. Maybe this is the nearest we come to the divine?

XXXII. I have wished to not be human, to slip from this world, turn saline—the rush of an ocean tide. For making sense of oneself and the world, reconciling to fear and love and hate, to a consistent lack of simplicity—this crux of being alive exhausts me.

XXXIII. But then I often feel my life is not my own, this body not my own—that this is all given to make something of, to fulfil, to repay—whom? A god? The gods? I do not know. Who does? Who on Earth truly understands what we are here for, what great drought and flood, what raining of plagues and reaching up, what earthquake and fire we are here to witness, to just, maybe, survive?

That Day the Haddock

It is said that the markings on either side of the haddock's head were left by the finger and thumb of Saint Peter, who, holding the fish's mouth agape, reached in and extracted a four-drachma coin from its gullet. That day, the haddock paid the temple tax of two men, which is to say, four days' wages.

In ancient Greece, burial customs dictated that a single coin be placed in the mouth of the deceased. Commonly an obol or danake coin, each possessed a value equivalent to one-sixth of a drachma— the market price of a sea urchin in the city of Athens. The coin, paid to Kharon, ferryman to Hades, ensured safe passage across the rivers Acheron and Styx.

In May of the year 1927, an Icelandic fisherman broke the world record when he hauled a three-foot-nine-inch haddock from the sea. Describing the specimen in his *General Features in the Biology of the Haddock (Gadus aeglefinus L.) in Icelandic Waters*, Harold

Thompson notes that the fish, thirteen to fourteen years in age, weighed an exceptional thirty-two pounds gutted. As the sale index of haddock hovered at half an Icelandic króna per pound, the fish held a market value of sixteen Icelandic króna. But its gullet—sliced across by a curved filleting knife—gaped coinless.

That day, unrivalled in size, the haddock paid but half the temple tax of one man, which is to say, seven crossings of the rivers Acheron and Styx, or, if one prefers, seven sea urchins smashed—slick, gelatinous, saline—from their casement of spines.

My Mother Photographs Me in
a Bath of Dead Squid

My mother always wanted me to look dead. Even when a car slammed my body against concrete, skull ricocheting off the kerbstone. When I woke to paramedics—*blood loss, suspected spinal, head blocks.* When the ambulance doors swung open as we took a roundabout, a paramedic grasping the stretcher, equipment hurtling out the back. As I was rushed into the emergency ward, my mother photographed me strapped to the spinal board, blood matting my hair, drenching my once-white Le Coq windbreaker. "No, don't wake up, look dead, Lars, look more dead."

*

"Open your eyes."

A mantle blurred into view. I sat up, gasped. The bathwater—littered with dead squid—veered, slapped soft bodies against ceramic. I blinked. "I can't open my eyes underwater. It stings."

"But I need you to look dead."

I untangled a tentacle from the plug chain. The water carried it—slack, filmy—past my torso.

"Lars, darling, the photos won't look right if you don't look dead."

"I'm cold."

"I can't add hot water. It'll affect the squid. Look, get under there, hold your breath, open your eyes. Come on, I haven't much film. And I can't waste this, I spent good money at that fishmonger's."

A fine art teacher, my mother led a yearly trip to Aberystwyth, Wales. During one of these trips, in the communal bathroom of a seafront B&B that hadn't seen an update since the fifties, my mother began a photography project that would span decades of my life. I have modelled in baths, glass cases, on beds, beaches, in forests. My body covered in dead fish, offal, dried flowers, ashes. My body cast, photographed, filmed, watched by gallery audience. My mother's instructions always: *Look dead, Lars, look more dead.*

I peered over the rim of the jaundiced tub at the rotten cork linoleum. My mother adjusted her weight, checked the light balance on her Nikon. A rancid odour lapped up from the dead squid. I could barely detect the cloying mix of bleach and antiseptic that announced the bathroom's cracked mirror and lacklustre tiling. I looked down at my legs, at the squid drifting against my shins. *Look dead, Lars, look more dead.* I inhaled, slipped below the water. Cold swallowed, blunted. I heard the muffled click of my mother photographing me, the squid. I waited one last moment, opened my eyes.

*

In the emergency ward, the nurse came in and saw my mother taking photos, telling me to open my eyes, close them again, look vacant, look dead. Dead, dead, dead.

"Do you want this woman escorted out?"

I lay on a stretcher in head blocks. The ceiling pulsed: "No, just the phone, get her to put the phone away."

"Madam—the phone."

"But I'm her mother."

Always that: *I'm her mother*. In supermarket aisles, in the car, on the street: *I shat you out my body like a melon, I can do what the fuck I want*. And even when a doctor poked at the glass and grit in my face, pushing so roughly that I breathed sharp. When another doctor saw this and lost his shit, medics rushing to pull the first "doctor" away from my body. When the actual physician explained that a psych patient sometimes stole a white coat and walked A&E pretending to be staff, even then, how I groaned, began to laugh, how my mother and I laughed. *Look more dead, Lars. Dead. Just look dead.*

*

For her funeral, my mother wants a black carriage drawn by black horses to carry her coffin down the high street. She wants a jazz band to follow in her wake, play "When the Saints Go Marching In" under the banner: "Music to Die For."

When I queried the cost and feasibility of the Victorian ceremony, my mother replied, "It is my dying wish." (She is not dying.) "You must do it or live with the guilt, because I won't be forgiving anyone. I'll be dead."

My mother recently said that she will have to record herself performing her own service, because no one else will do it with sufficient passion.

On this point, I am inclined to agree.

*

For the remainder of our time in Aberystwyth, no one used the bathroom my mother co-opted for the photo shoot. The stench of dead squid had anyone gagging barely two minutes into brushing their teeth. For the entire week, three floors of guests filed round the stairwell, waiting for a ten-minute spot in the establishment's only other bathroom. Waiting there, towel flopped over her forearm, my mother decided to move the project outside of the B&B. The next three days, she photographed me in rock pools, lying face down on the sand. In one negative, molluscs line my back. In another, a severed salmon head rests beside my own.

*

In Sophie Calle's *Voir la mer / See the Sea*, 2011, inhabitants of Istanbul who have never beheld an ocean are driven to the shores of the Black Sea. Calle films them from behind as they unmask their eyes to take in the shoreline. When they are ready, they turn around to face the camera: Eyes charged with the sight of wild water. Bodies seen and seeing. Tangled dynamic of artistic means and subject.

*

My mother drank hard, laughed hard, spoke hard. She spent money she didn't have, said things she didn't mean. She didn't cook, swore by TV dinners, and most certainly did not think everything I did was wonderful. She preferred the phrase "What are you tit arsing around at?" to "How was your day, darling?" When I brought home school projects or "bits of twonky shite" as she referred to them, she did not pretend they deserved a place on any living room shelf, but simply took them off my hands, exclaiming, "God, what am I meant to do with this gobshite?" Quickly followed by: "I mean, darling, it's *lovely*," all uttered in the single movement of project to pedal bin.

My mother never wanted a homemade gift or a hand-drawn card: "Don't be cheap, have the decency to buy me something that's not an eyesore."

She is not a conventionally "good" mother. But then, put like that, it sounds like a slow death sentence anyhow.

*

England, midwinter 2005. An unheated art studio. Modelling for a recumbent full-body plaster cast.

In the abandoned toilet block, snow obscured the awning window. My breath misted the mirror. A pipe dripped. The tube light—its plastic casement pitted with dead moths—flickered. The weather could not have been worse for a plaster cast. I snapped a swim cap over my hair and ears. I undressed. My feet settled upon cold, gritty tiling. Days before Christmas, the building stood empty, cavernous. I retrieved a tub of Vaseline from my bag and applied a layer to my face, arms, underarms, stomach, and groin. I smeared the Vaseline over my eyebrows and eyelashes, held on to the sink, blinked.

Prior to a plaster cast, bodily hair must be greased with petroleum jelly. The difficulty lies in never applying so much as to obscure the patterning of the skin—pores, scars, individual hairs—as this gives a high-quality finish and realism to the cast. But too little and the removal of the cast could turn into a slow, full-body wax.

The technician knocked on the toilet block door. "You ready?"

"Just the clingfilm to go."

"I'll wait, let me know if you need help."

As a child, I always wore legging shorts for modesty when being cast. But as the fabric absorbs the liquid plaster, the shorts bind to the cast, meaning one has to be cut out of them. Unlike cotton underwear or shorts, clingfilm repels liquid plaster, preventing the removal of pubic hair or the irritation of sensitive skin.

Pulling a roll of Glad Wrap from my bag, I stretched it over my genitals and taped it in place. I opened the door. "Ready to party."

*

Between the ages of four and nineteen, I modelled for:

>Thirteen full-body casts: ten plaster, two Sellotape, one tissue.
>Three performance pieces: bed, wake, autopsy table.
>Four short films: one in which I sleep with eight others on a wall of scaffolding; a second that shows me surfacing from a bath of black water, gasping on repeat; another whereby I walk in wax shoes until they shatter underfoot; and another still in which I wear paper clothing as buckets of water are dumped over me.

Across those fifteen years, my mother collected:

>Eight animal skulls: lion, alligator, water buffalo, bison, horse, camel, cat, monkey.
>One framed set of Victorian wax dental casts.
>Three life-size anatomical models.
>A turn-of-the-century glass eye (blue).
>Two articulated skeletons: pigeon, frog.
>A taxidermy seagull.
>A child's shoe retrieved from a bog, the mud having preserved its leather and laces since the Middle Ages.

The time we visited Florida, my mother purchased a second suitcase so as to accommodate the shells, coral, shark jaws, snakeskin wallets, and sea sponges she'd bought. The 1940s rowing oars required a more elaborate persuasion of air staff.

Customs was never a quick affair.

*

If my mother found a dead animal, she would place the corpse in a carrier bag and head home to bury it in the backyard.

Six months later, flesh and fur and feathers decomposed in earth, she'd dig up the skeleton.

We did this whilst drinking lemonade, Diet Coke.

*

My aunt once helped my mother with a photography project. My mother wrapped her in layers of clingfilm in the heartland of British suburbia that is my grandmother's back garden. It was midsummer. Each day clung stickily to the next. My aunt, sweltering, fainted. My mother tore her from the plastic as my grandmother marched out of the kitchen: "What on earth will the neighbours think?" As her forty-year-old younger daughter revived, staggering naked between plastic lawn chairs, a group of dog walkers looked on from the meadow beyond the garden wall. At this, my grandmother reached her limit: "Even the Labradors are staring."

*

Another year, my mother dried flowers by laying them over the living room floorboards, until we had to jump from one vacant foothold to another. The postman caught sight of me, once, performing this intricate ballet from sofa to kitchen kettle, and I shrugged, not seeing what was so strange about any of it.

*

A fan heater wheezed across the studio's herringbone floor.

"This is all we've got," my mother turned from a boiling kettle, "the other heater's packed up. You still okay to do this?"

"I'll manage."

Black sugar paper covered the casting studio's windows. Bulbs hummed overhead, shivered light onto a laminated table. On the table, two basins stood beside pre-cut piles of plaster bandage. My mother filled the basins with boiling water, adding a glass of cold to make it workable.

"Right, last calls: lavatory, Vaseline? Anything else you need?"

"No, I'm good."

Full-body casts run at high cost—studio space, technicians, models, materials. They also require considerable time and logistical coordination. Needing to urinate or defecate during the casting process will cost an artist hundreds of dollars and hours of their time. The cast will have to be abandoned—unfinished, unusable. The night and morning before a cast, I eat plain rice or pasta and drink as little as possible. I also, prior to applying Vaseline or clingfilm, pass a hot washcloth over my face, neck, and chest. The body will soon be cold and covered in warm, wet bandage. The washcloth preemptively triggers any need to urinate induced by temperature difference.

I lifted myself onto the table, lay on my side. My mother and the technician adjusted my limbs.

"Bring the arms into the chest, that's it. Now, this arm, lay that atop the other, but not perfectly. Yes, off-centre. And the fingers—don't separate them; they'll be too fragile once cast. Maybe bring the knees up. Can you work on that space across the stomach, between the thighs and the arms?"

The technician clicked on a paint-smattered radio. Static hazed, settled over my collarbone, my ribcage. My mother wetted a strip of two-by-two-inch plaster bandage, pulled it between forefingers to remove excess moisture, and smoothed it onto my skin. Rubbing the wet bandage, she distributed the plaster of Paris across the webbing. The technician repeated the process along my feet. Christmas hits whined from the radio. The smell of plaster eddied off my body—mild, powdery. I closed my eyes, exhaled.

A full-body cast, performed by two people using plaster bandage, takes around three hours—work speed and ambient temperature depending. That midwinter day, with temperatures groaning below zero, with a team of only my mother and one technician, the cast would take four and a half hours. Curled on my side, the majority of my weight fell on my hip and shoulder. After only fifteen minutes, my body ached. The cast would prove one of the most demanding I would ever endure.

*

After my parents separated, I lived alone with my mother from the age of four until I left home at eighteen. We rarely ate together, instead using the dining table to assemble photographs, severed talons, wings. In the evenings, we read or worked in separate rooms. The bathroom was different.

My mother says that the best thing I ever did for the house was to put a chair in the bathroom. Whilst this might suggest just how little I did for the home—a sentiment my mother would back—I'd like to think it also points to how we used that room. To the late-night talk, words clouding vaporous in steaming heat. How, at hours of disjoint from work and routine, we were able to relinquish something more honest of ourselves, one of us bathing, the other sat listening as thoughts fell into water. How it has always been in a bathroom that my mother and I find an understanding. How water—crashing, stilling, water carrying a body exhausted—how it engenders a rare generosity.

*

My grandmother tells stories of my mother as a teenager deciding to dress "as an artist," which is to say, sporting two flannelette dressing gowns beneath a cape to the grocers, or a fur coat held together by some thirty safety pins to church. Regardless, my grandmother made her elder daughter walk several paces behind her.

*

When, at two years old, I learnt the word *no* and screamed it every time someone tried to put me in a dress, a girl's bathing costume, a girl's T-shirt, shorts, underwear, anything pink or pretty, my mother only stood back and said, "This kid's as queer as they come." She watched as I picked out boys' toys—cork guns, plastic swords, Action Men, Mighty Max, a boy's twenty-one gear bike. Watched as I chose boxer shorts, green nylon swim trunks, as the hairdresser handed me a magazine and I turned and turned the pages until there was a picture of a man advertising perfume, until I pointed to his crew cut, looking warily upwards to see if it would be approved.

*

The bathroom back home is smallish and hasn't seen a renovation in decades. The doorknob crashes off the door. The tub lies scrubbed of enamel. A bullet hole fractures the window from the night when a neighbour shot an air rifle at the lit pane, my mother's silhouetted body stepping out of range by seconds. Paint peels from the floorboards. There's no shower, only a rubber mixer head that hangs, limp, from the bath taps. A bathroom accessory so 1950s in style that my mother is perpetually worried Boots will stop carrying it. The tiling—a 1970s beige-brown stripe—frames all this across two walls, wavers beneath the single, hesitant bulb. It is the one room we've never had the money to redecorate.

When I think of my mother, it is almost always of her in this room with its copper boiler that takes two hours to heat, in this room holding out against all odds, her shoulders rounded in the tub, water rippling over her limbs.

In the time we've spent in the bathroom, mirrors fogged with steam, a sliver of light spilling round the doorframe from the landing, my mother has told me she's tired, no, really tired, my love; she's voiced her fears, consistently asked for and ignored my advice; she's recounted who's engaged or pregnant or getting divorced at work; she's told me we're in debt, that the house needs remortgaging a third time; that she wants to do an installation piece of nine sleeping women and will I participate? She has asked what the fuck I'm playing around at, told me I'm making a mistake. Usually, I come back and tell her she was right, maybe it takes a night or several years, but she's almost always right. It's a strange thing to acknowledge: that your mother knows you better than you know yourself.

*

I do not remember the physiological changes of puberty, do not recall developing breasts or hips. They all remain things that my body renders thankfully impossible to excavate. But I do remember my mother telling me that I'd find a way, in this skin, find a way to articulate the body as tension, as contradiction. How, with time, these edges might even cohere—brief flickering of moth to light.

*

My mother, a woman who in childhood photographs looks like a boy. A woman who, at university after another student was murdered in her building, shaved her head and wore men's clothing. A woman who frequently passed as male. A woman who once said to me, "If times had been different, I'd have turned out like you."

*

I came out as queer whilst my mother drew a bath.
  "Fucking *finally*," she said.
  She spun the faucet fully open, water collapsing upon water.
  "Thank God we don't have to play along with that anymore."

*

The technician dried her hands on a chequered rag. She took a pair of scissors, cut a plastic straw into short lengths. Modroc covered my entire body except my face. The radio wavered—dull, indistinct, distant. My body shivered. Pain seared across my hips, ribs, shoulders. I controlled the urge to shudder.

"Almost there, my love."

My mother emptied, refilled the basins.

The technician crouched to my eye level: "We're going to cover the forehead, eyes, and jaw now. I'll let you know when we're starting the mouth. After that, it'll be one sound for *yes*, two for *no*. All right?"

Steam rose off the basins, warped the light.

"Okay, Lars, close your eyes."

As plaster bandage layered across my eyelids, the reddish glow of backlit blood extinguished. Darkness swelled.

I heard the technician's voice near my ear. "Mouth now."

I closed my lips, made a noise in my throat. The technician slowly inserted a section of plastic straw in each nostril.

"Can you breathe?"

Noise in my throat.

The radio slurred into the darkness. Plaster stung my eyes, itched my mouth. Air rattled—thin, weak—through the straws. The metal legs of a stool dragged across the floor. A kettle boiled. Spoons clinked against mugs.

"An hour's drying time to go, Lars."

There is a moment during a full-body plaster cast, after several layers of Modroc have been applied, after the eye sockets and mouth have been sealed into darkness, when only two nostril holes or a straw between the lips feed your breathing, a moment when you panic—even after thirteen casts and accustomed to the process.

I counted, slowed my breathing.

*

When I was fourteen, an autopsy table retailed at £1,000. My mother sold off antiques and flipped through pages of beds, stretchers, and stainless-steel tables in a medical supplies catalogue. One week later, an "Autopsy Table ST 10/500 Moveable" was ours.

For three separate performance pieces, I lay on the table, my body partially covered by a white sheet. Some twelve hours in total. My mother announced the project as a doctor might recommend a cure: "Half a day's death to temper your youth, it'll do you a power of good."

*

I flexed my face muscles—the plaster tugged at my eyelashes. I flexed again. My eyelids peeled from the cast. Eyelashes tore from their ducts. I rolled my lips, tasted blood as plaster rent skin. I breathed within heavy carapace. The cast compressed my ribcage, my back, my throat, my cheeks.

"Lars, we're almost there. The plaster needs another twenty minutes. Can you hold on?"

My body struggled to convulse, to vomit. I breathed through the straws—slow, insipid. My eyes watered. My nose ran. My body shivered.

"Lars?"

A cast cures by leaching the model's body heat. It rigidifies, shrinks. The cast increasingly restricts the chest cavity, forcing a slow, shallow kind of breathing. Yet, amidst this, one must maintain a state of absolute immobility, of perfect stasis. *Look dead, Lars, look more dead.*

*

Aged four and modelling for my first full-body cast, I screamed when the technicians plastered over my eyes and mouth, screamed so fiercely that the technicians had to rip the plaster from my face and remove the rest of the cast early.

Thinking I was going to suffocate, I shouted for the technicians to "get the fucking bastard thing off me." The technicians all agreed: "Definitely your kid, Sheri."

*

Another time, during my twenties, my mother asked last minute if I could come to her exhibition opening earlier than arranged. I apologised: I worked, otherwise I would have. The next day, I arrived at the gallery. Pushing through the doors, I found my mother lying naked in a vitrine of offal and maggots. The maggots seethed through her hair, crawled over her face, between toes, fingers, over her stomach.

She calls it a scheduling error. I call it divinely ordained escape.

The irony is, had she simply explained that she needed a model for maggots and entrails, I'd have called in sick to work. I doubt it's even a lie when one spends the day beneath heaped, rotting death.

*

Years later, when my mother learnt that the woman I would eventually marry was not only a writer—a career of which she approved— but also Puerto Rican, she couldn't have been happier: "Puerto Rico has the most exceptional funerals; the extreme embalming there is an art. You know, Lars, I thought about having you done that way, if ever you died first."

Only in death would my mother ever have me model as alive.

*

One tends to imagine bodily sensation increasing as the modelling process progresses: how levels of physical discomfort rise due to cramps and muscle fatigue, how extremes of temperature seem to escalate. And yet, even if I experienced this early on, even though I still contend with discomfort during casts, performances, and film-photography shoots, so often, modelling is a way through, even past discomfort. Odours dissipate. The fetid loses its aversion. Maggots, flies, butchered meat—all cease to cause repulsion. The body can accommodate. Become a thing of changing dimensions. Of breadth. Space in which the world can rearticulate.

*

In Rachel Whiteread's *One Hundred Spaces*, 1995, the vacuous undersides of one hundred chairs are rendered solid, cast in bright, gummy-like resin. The sculptural forms—cuboid, the occasional concave scroll of a former spindle—stand in regimented lines. I remember a description saying they were all taken from the undersides of bathroom stools. Now that I look again, years later, I can only find it listed as chairs. I wonder if that was ever true or if I only imagined them as bathroom stools, subconsciously saw those strangely aqueous objects as echoes. The river of one's own life sweeping outwards, swallowing anything within reach.

*

Even in my teens, when my mother drank heavily, when I would draw the bath for her near midnight, help wash her back as I placed pint after pint of water on the rim for her to drink, even when I made sure she dried off, put on pyjamas, got safely to bed, we still talked. Even if she was drunk, she told me how and why she wasn't coping, the job, money, raising me, how everything was veering, not working out right.

It was also in that bathtub, years later, that my mother returned the favour after I had a breakdown, after I stopped talking, my back a wreck of torn muscle tissue, my body swollen, lethargic. Decades since she'd last helped me wash, she soaped my skin, told me this would pass, not to worry, that of course I'd think and read and write again, that I'd not always be dependent. Only years later did she admit that she feared I'd never get back to myself.

She washed my hair, my face. My mother, not known for her sentimentality. Once, a friend phoned, said, "Sheri, my husband's been having an affair, I think we're getting a divorce." My mother replied, "Okay, my baked potato's just cooked, so I'll eat that and phone you afterwards." My mother, who will eat her dinner before listening to your heartache. This woman carried me that year, knelt at the bathtub to wash me, sat next to me as I hyperventilated on the bedroom, the living room, on any and every available floor.

My mother gives her best advice in the bathroom. She'll tell me when I've fucked up, when a situation is or isn't my fault. She'll tell me how the book she's reading really does put my situation in perspective, and it's often true because medieval plague and superviruses and the minds of serial killers do have a knack of doing that. She tells me when to get my shit together. Most of all, though, not to be too hard on myself when it all goes arse over tit, because it will, because it has to if you are to live.

*

When I tell people about growing up with my mother their responses usually fall somewhere between disbelief, humour, and concern. As for how I felt: I remember arriving at university, this supposedly wild and exciting time of one's life, and realising a few weeks in that never had my life been so ordinary, never had I been so perfectly, painfully bored.

*

Barring performance art, society tends to understand artwork as the static end product of a creative process. As terminal object, relic. As artefact. Objects to which we come in temporal reverse. I am most interested in artwork as creative process. In the dynamics that occur before, and up to, any final outcome. I like the slipperiness of that. Revising, refining, hauling to surface. The physical effort, bodily gesture. I want the slow plasticity of binding action into object. Collisions of body and media. Physicality collapsing into physicality.

*

There is something about bathrooms that approaches modelling. The stasis. Being in one's skin, differently. A room of water. Of piped current. The particular kind of intimacy—with oneself, others. How water carries a body. Takes time, memory, takes physicality within the tide of itself.

*

After some four hours, my mother slid a hand between the cast and my skin. She pushed into my back, my thighs, drew a thumb along my calf. I made small movements, lost hair, bled. I emerged cramped, shaking, bruised. The technician supported my weight as I staggered, legs folding, to the toilet washbasin. The technician held me as my body juddered, applied a warm washcloth to the bruising that stretched from my thigh to my ribs. For the next hour, I collapsed.

The bodily depletion after an extensive cast defies easy category. The lack of coordination. The inability to immediately regain autonomy. Muscle seizure. Blood seething up the arms and legs. This strange reacquaintance with movement, temperature, with sound. A shaking of death from limb. The instability of something newly birthed.

*

Photographs make me uncomfortable. The frontal smiling. To fashion oneself, pose. But to have one's body curated, articulated and placed. To have it arranged in unfamiliar ways. I like that. How it forces me to feel my body differently. Its strange pace. To hold the body in stasis, duration leadening the limbs with new weight. To feel the shifting texture as one occupies space. I like the estrangement of modelling. And its strangeness.

Being transmasculine, my body largely resists feelings of owner-ship. The sensation of waking within limbs that one recognises, of finding oneself reflected, to sense propriety over one's body—I have never felt that. I am still surprised, even after thirty years of living in this skin, when I catch sight of myself in mirrors. It still manages to come as a slap of cold water in the early-morning light. I experience my body as vessel, as carrier, as God-given, perhaps. Bearer of a dis-jointed entity—watery thing that doesn't fit the body I walk within. Maybe that is why modelling sits comfortably with me: my body rarely feels like my own, anyhow. I am grateful for my body, for how it moves me through the world, but I do experience it as distance, as transient shell that I will walk out of in the same way I walked in. I identify with the gazes put upon it. Their exteriority. To look *at* myself more than *as* myself. To experience oneself from within, but also, crucially, from without.

As for the Tilapia

But, of course, Saint Peter never did extract a coin from the mouth of the haddock, a species entirely foreign to the Sea of Galilee. Nor did he, as other sources claim, clasp his hand around the John Dory, whose yellowish flanks carry a single black mark—known colloquially as the fish's "evil eye." As for the tilapia, however, a fish populating the River Jordan for millennia—this could well be Saint Peter's true catch.

Long before biblical times, the ancient Egyptians believed the tilapia protected the sun god, Ra, piloting his boat in its daily journey around the sky's arc. Thus, in the Egyptian *Book of the Dead*, the fish appears as an omen of rebirth, cresting alongside Ra's solar barque—the vessel by which dead souls journeyed to the afterlife. Harbinger and guardian, the tilapia navigated between worlds of health and sickness, life and death, swam from Earth to firmament, and back again.

Last Night, a Doctor Handed Me a Glass of Water

XXXIV.   A ghost knifefish—juvenile, black, electric—curled at its base.

According to native Amazonian belief, the deceased inhabit the ghost knifefish after death, souls sifting through riverbeds, creeks, suddenly luminous, searing apart the deep.

Νάρκη (nárkē): ancient Greek to mean *torpedo fish, electric ray*, but also *numbness, stupor, pain relief.* An etymology shared with narcotics.

Swallow the fish.

XXXV.   Miami, Florida, USA, 2019: Water deluged. Sheet rain hammered the asphalt, flooded the guttering. Wind beat palms, bowing them over cars. Another day of geckos under vending machines, parrots huddled in doorways, another day of animals scoured from sky and earth. Under the heavy purple of dawn, I drove to the local pool. As I stepped inside the gate, water sluicing off my neck, lightning split the night, blessed me, the lifeguard, one other lone swimmer in blinding light. The lifeguard looked at the clouds: "¡Se te aguó el día! Rain's okay, but lightning—we'll have to close." Driving back to the apartment, my T-shirt clinging to my arms and chest, I took Ocean Drive—a road normally gridlocked, now abandoned, gaping beneath thunderous sky. A taxi seared through the dark beside me; far off, the ocean bruised. That day, supermarkets haemorrhaged tins and bottled water as hurricane warnings flashed across television sets: two, three, suspected category four, then—five, evacuation advisable.

XXXVI. The afternoon already drowning, I packed a bag and drove north. Signs crowded the highway: *NO GAS. SHOP ONLY. EMPTY!* Some three hours from Miami, I reached the only place for miles with petrol. Tailbacks blocked the gas station entrance, clogging the motorway. At one pump, a man in a string vest filled canister after canister as other cars honked, rolled down windows: "Stop that shit!" "Pendejo, move on!" For the next four hours, the car radio crackling traffic announcements, I drove into the gaining night. I remember the rain fell so heavily it acted like fog, car headlamps smudging across the asphalt. And the palms—blown so violently as to be caught in the breath of a god.

XXXVII. "FOR NEPTUNE HIMSELF IS CALLED THE GENERATOR. And the race of Hellen sacrificed to

Neptune as the first father, imagining, as likewise the Syrians did, that man rose from a liquid substance. . . . [However, Anaximander] says that fish and men were not produced in the same substances, but that men were first produced in fishes, and, when they were grown up and able to help themselves, were thrown out, and so lived upon the land."

—Plutarch, *Quaestiones convivales*

XXXVIII. Past a certain age, my own reflection became increasingly difficult to look at. So, I didn't. I looked out. Around. At others. Animals. Trees. Anything not myself. And if one does this for long enough, seeks solace in this breathing, rolling earth, how much of one's supposedly "internal" self becomes exploded, more forcibly, more tangibly than most? To live through the world, see oneself better in its rivers, lakes, cliffs, in the arc of migrating birds, schooling fish. To better grasp oneself in slow tides, waters eddying along darkened shoreline.

XXXIX. I am finding it hard to address myself so directly. To wade back into this water of childhood. Of a body that seemed to betray me. Or that I simply struggled to keep up with, to understand as rapidly as it needed. How does one write of a self that is fundamentally displaced? Of a self that, for decades, has seen and not recognised its own body?

XL. As a child, I screamed if anything female touched my skin. I attended boys' youth groups, played on boys' sports teams. But, at around nine or ten, clubs began to tell me I couldn't attend, girls stared at me in changing rooms. A body I had been so comfortable

in, grew unfamiliar. Nothing fit. By the time I arrived in secondary school, aged eleven, I stuck out:
"What is it?"

XLI.   I began presenting as feminine, cisgender, heterosexual to avoid getting shoved every six feet in the
school corridor, to sit in a classroom and not have
people call you "he-she," "dyke." I conformed so as
to make it through a comprehensive school where
one boy would pretend to fuck furniture each lesson;
where kids would come in saying they'd had a great
holiday, because they'd broken into a building and
taken a shit on a table together; a school where one
boy beat another until blood ran thick in the corridor,
teachers and students sliding over linoleum, blood
smattering shoes, trousers, fists. I worked, counted
down the years. I left.

XLII.   I wished I could slough myself—the versions people
preferred, where I conformed, presented as female,
heterosexual. Hand those out, let them filmily talk
and do and be, so that my real self, my truest, strange
slip of a body could walk more peacefully, alone, but
at ease. If my body could have lied without killing
me, maybe I would have.

XLIII.   I knew myself better at six, at eight, at ten, than I did at
eighteen, twenty-three. Only in my late twenties did
I return to a self I had asphyxiated for over a decade.
When you've withdrawn so far, when you've watched,
actively encouraged something within you to die, suffocate under some algal bloom of a defence—it takes
time to resuscitate a self, a life you've endeavoured
to forget.

XLIV.   There are many things I might have done differently: hormone blockers, testosterone, surgery. But which child gets that life? Which ten-year-old is entrusted with their own body? Trusted to know it with a maturity beyond their years, beyond anyone's understanding. The soul—fleck of a god and fading. Which ten-year-old is given the sheer freedom to request medical assistance to alter their own physiognomy? None that I know.

XLV.   I don't reproach anyone for not seeing I was trans as a kid. I don't reproach myself for not speaking up. I have never been one to voice things. I've always been more action-based, more watery. My body speaks more than my mouth.

XLVI.   Growing up, I didn't think my parents, family, or friends either understood or could understand—that I felt uncomfortable in my skin, that I had always been male. Or other, both. But now, looking back, I think everyone understood. In the way that truth settles over a body in the small hours, undisturbed by the screech of cars, by the dull hum of rent and bills and groceries, in that quiet, dark way, I think everyone understood who I was, who I still am.

XLVII.   Looking again at the childhood photograph of me in Florida, tank at my back, I admire the simplicity of the shark. A body of sheer muscle. To move with instinct, clear intent. Perhaps, at that point, I still had a sense of myself that existed simply—not overly impeded by my body's physical changes or society's expectations of me. Perhaps, on some small level, I felt common ground.

XLVIII. Both of us captive: the shark in its tank, and me unable to pull out of this body, this being human. Someone no one else quite sees. Our bodies glowing green
light. Inches from one another. Resonance rippling
through reinforced acrylic.

XLIX. In AD 1369, the Chinese emperor Hongwu, founder
of the Ming dynasty, rebuilt the imperial porcelain manufactory at Jingdezhen—an unusual prior-
ity only two years into one's reign, but a fortuitous
one where aquariums are concerned. Amongst its
numerous ornaments, the imperial porcelain manu-
facture produced basins or "fishbowls." One such
example survives in the form of a large, lobed bowl:
hatched and stippled in several washes of cobalt,
carp, Chinese perch, and two varieties of bream
swim between lotuses, clover fern, feathered pond-
weed. Dating to the fifth Ming emperor Xuande's
reign (AD 1425–AD 1435), the piece was auctioned
by Sotheby's in 2017 for 229,037,500 Hong Kong dollars, the equivalent of 29,552,310 US dollars.

L. By AD 1554, the Ming dynasty's court, then under the
rule of the Jiajing emperor, ordered an impressive list
of porcelain ornaments from the Jingdezhen factory.
Fishbowls are not only requested in high quantity, but
arrive fourth on a nine-item list:

FOR THE THIRTY-THIRD YEAR OF
CHIA-CHING (A.D. 1554):

Bowls (Wan), 26,350, with a blue ground, decorated
with a pair of dragons in clouds.
Plates (Tieh), 30,500, of the same design.

Wine-Cups (Chan), 6,900, white inside, blue outside, with the typical flowers of the four seasons.
Large Fish-Bowls (Yü Kang), 680, decorated with blue flowers on a white ground.
Teacups (Ou), 9,000, with foliated rims, of greenish white (*ch'ing pai*) or celadon porcelain.
Bowls (Wan), 10,200, decorated outside with lotus flowers, fish, and water plants, painted in blue on a white ground; inside, upon a blue ground, with dragons and phoenixes passing through flowers, and with a band of dragons and flowers round the rim.
Teacups (Ou), 19,800, of the same pattern.
Libation Cups (Chüeh), 600, with hill-shaped saucers (*shau-p'an*) to support the three feet, of blue color, decorated with sea-waves and a pair of dragons in clouds.
Wine-Pots or Ewers (Hu), 6,000, of white porcelain.

—Stephen W. Bushell, *Oriental Ceramic Art:*
Illustrated by Examples from the
Collection of W. T. Walters

LI.   From the half-barrel tubs of the late fourteenth century to the basins and ever more rounded bowls of the 1700s, Chinese porcelain fishbowls increasingly resembled the spherical glass tanks that would eventually succeed them as the iconic home aquarium.

LII. Savannah, Georgia, USA, 2019: That evening, after driving miles from Miami, hurricane warnings blaring out of cars, gas station radios, I lay back on a hotel bed. Maps glared across the TV, lit the walls in wind speeds, pulsing red warnings. Surrounded by polyester furnishings, rain hammering the panes, I watched Savannah's city council announce a mandatory evacuation for the following day. One night's rest, then onwards. I picked my phone off the bedside table, its screen glowing with the childhood photograph. Me, the shark, Florida some twenty years ago. I decided to head for Atlanta in the morning, spend the day at the Georgia Aquarium milling through blue water, electric-coloured life.

LIII.   I thought back to that family holiday in Florida, to the week we spent on Sanibel Island, a tropical storm raging for days. How the waters flooded the streets, seeped into parked cars, slapped over nylon-upholstered seats. On the third day, a workman came to repair the television set in our holiday let. I remembered watching him from the window. How, one-armed, chewing tobacco, he flung open the doors of his van, three hounds growling amongst the cables and bent antennae. How, once he'd got the signal back, he smoked and spat over our balcony, told my mother not to worry, rain screaming down, "This is nothing here, just sit tight, you'll be fine." And my mother afterwards, not sure whether to believe this man or take him as a harbinger of the apocalypse.

The Conviction of Things Not Seen

Found deep beneath the ice floes of Arctic waters, the Greenland shark grows up to twenty-four feet in length, moves at a maximum speed of 1.7 miles per hour, and feeds mainly on sunken carcasses.

Only reaching maturity at 150 years of age, the species possesses the longest known lifespan among vertebrates.

But with 90 percent of Greenland sharks carrying a parasite on their corneas, the animal must swim blind for life—some three to five centuries.

Under the Fishes

As they fled Typhon—creature of fishtails and bloodlust—Aphrodite and her son Eros transformed into fishes, burying themselves in the Euphrates riverbed. So impressed was Zeus that he lifted the fishes from the river and cast them into the firmament. Two bright bodies joined by flaming cord: one swims for heaven, the other orbits Earth's horizon.

One of the earliest constellations on record, Pisces is referenced as far back as 10,000 BC in Ratnagiri petroglyphs and appears again in 2300 BC, the tied fishes inscribed upon an Egyptian coffin lid. Traditionally ruled by Jupiter—the most beneficent body in the sky, a planet of faith, breadth, and blessings—and, more recently, by Neptune—planet of dreams, poetry, and psychic ability—Pisces occupies the "House of the Unconscious," presides over beginnings and endings, the disintegration and renewal of matter. Also known as ruler of the "House of Reckoning," the Fishes are a sign under which one's actions must be weighed, must be washed in the sky's waters.

Owing to this eternal water over limbs—bodies slack, submerged, rinsed—ancient medical belief upheld Pisces as a curative sign, one of hospices and healing, the Fishes cosmically presiding over sickness of the veins and feet. Over channels of blue current. Long lost caudal fins.

*

Mont Noir, Franco-Belgian border, 2007: Commercial units spluttered hand-painted signs, slashed price tags: *TABAC, ALCOOLS, CUIR—DISCOUNT, PRIX BELGES.* Neon glowed into the night: *FRITES, BIÈRES, GAUFFRES, CRÊPES.* In the distance, bulbs blinked the outline of a martini glass above an imitation American nightclub as Johnny Halliday reverberated off panelled mirror, words caught in sweeping red-green, in shuddering strobe lights.

Except for weekends, when French locals crossed the border to load their cars with cheap beer and cigarettes, Mont Noir drew few visitors, the border tourist spot long past its prime. But, even as I cycled home after a late shift, the front generator lamp wheezing dim-bright with the tyre movement, there was always the flare of neon, the smell of fat hissing over hot metal to warm the night.

I worked illegally in the kitchens, rinsing beer glasses, mopping floors, and scrubbing meat chambers—a task that took two hours, turned my lips blue, and left a ferrous taste—ringing—in my mouth.

Eighteen, just out of sixth form, and not yet at university, I'd left home to teach English in La Vendée, France. I quit the job a few months in, after living with a family that spent every waking hour screaming at each other, a family so beyond my own parents' means it was uncomfortable, a family that threw dinner parties of Bellinis and coquilles Saint Jacques, during which everyone miraculously got along, only to then revert to a strict diet of arguments and slimming shakes. After an older male teacher invited me sightseeing, tried to grope me that evening. After the other teachers, asking if he'd tried again and I'd said, "No, not yet," shrugged: "Well, that's okay then." After I sat up one night and realised that I had enjoyed three evenings during the entire three months.

That January, my papers expired, I took a train to the Belgian border, a place where the rain never quite let up, where the work came and went as much as the staff.

I was suffering from a skin ailment. Verrucae covered the sole of my right foot, multiplied despite extraction by liquid nitrogen and curved surgical scissors, despite the constant smell of iodine and salt salves wound in ironed cloth.

It was during this time of endless glassware, the smell of beer mixing uncomfortably with that of melting sugar and fat fryers, this time of rinsing animal blood from stainless steel, the hum of strip lights and an industrial fan whirring overhead, that a man told me my destiny was to move towards water.

Each morning, I clicked on the electric bar heater, drew a shallow bath, amber light crashing into the tub. I removed the dressing of cotton wadding soaked in cider vinegar, covered the skin with duct tape. Colourless, bloated, dangling outside the bathtub as I washed, my foot resembled dead meat.

I used to think a lot of Don Thompson, the British racewalker who took gold at the 1960 Rome Olympics. In a steamed bathroom, he trained for the Italian climate by walking on a treadmill bundled in layers, a paraffin heater hissing at his feet. Don Thompson used to get dizzy after thirty minutes of training. He thought it was the temperature, but later realised it was due to carbon monoxide fumes from the heater.

Shallow warmth. Single-blade razor. Bar soap. I dried off with a hand towel unravelling at every edge, and dressed—gym shorts, T-shirt, tracksuit top, a shredded pair of Gola Flyers, the right shoe worn loose with two pairs of socks.

I struggled to walk on the lacerated skin of my right foot, but I could cycle. Every morning, I rose before anyone else, cycled through fields, the sun knifing hard and cold over frostbitten earth. I passed the same villagers, each of us bound in the strings of our own life: One woman, an apron tied about her gingham dress, pegged washing to the line. Some days, she beat a rug, threw scrap meat to a pair of Dobermanns. Further along, an elderly man smoked in the doorway, dressed in a sleeveless undershirt despite the January cold.

Depending on the day, I might cycle to Mont Rouge, Mont Kemmel, or even to the Belgian town of Ypres, where a widow kept an antiques shop of glass flower-domes and nineteenth-century children's shoes. But I always made sure to climb the Mont-des-Cats, pay my respects to the Trappist abbey that loomed above the landscape, silence lapping off its brickwork.

I paused at the top of the hill, the abbey at my back. My lungs strained after an ascent that saw tourists reverse their cars and re-attempt the climb at high speed. Below, the fields stretched far and flat—muddied landscape of whispering ground.

Each summer, monks and nuns visited my Catholic school in the hope that one of us had heard God above the din of TVs and Discmans, that the divine might finally be chatting on Hotmail Messenger this year. Everyone else I knew had always laughed off those visits. I never felt as convinced. On Mont-des-Cats, I stood beneath the monastery, weighed what I'd foregone against what awaited—obscurity against obscurity. To leave this world and take the veil. To vow oneself to silence, devotions of blessed oil and frankincense. To toil, commit one's body to the brewing of hops or churning of milk, the construction of coffins for public use. During those months on the border, I struggled to fathom myself: who I was, what I wanted. What lay ahead seemed the roll and sweep of some chaotic current—unruly happenstance. But, looking back, I wonder whether, even when a self blurs, when paths chosen reveal themselves misguided, if one's vocation—this dark and nebulous navigation—if it occurs as the nuns always said: soft, reverberating, a faraway tide that comes calling. Imperceptible yet guiding. If that is the definition of a god.

*

My landlord worked as a secretary in an abattoir. Each day, I returned once she'd left for work. Wheeling the bike into the basement, I ducked under lines of laundry hung between car parts, edged my way around tools, spare tyres, and a blown-out TV set that was permanently "going to be repaired." I peeled the clothes from my body and washed in the basement's stand-to shower, a thirty-watt bulb glowing weak over mildewed plastic.

During the day, I sat at the local library, leafed through out-of-date editions of *L'Équipe* and a copy of Marguerite Yourcenar's *Mémoires d'Hadrien*, the dictionary at my right. I'd check my email on the single PC—the internet connection an old dial tone, screeching dust off the shelves. Opening hours were slim in that town, starved even. Once the library closed at 3:00 p.m., I'd sleep a stretch before work. When I couldn't sleep, I'd visit the colombophile.

A retired rail worker, Jean-Marie padded about the house in slippers, busied himself with either his birds or the garden. When I knocked, he'd usher me down the hall to the kitchen, insist I sit on the vinyl bench as he brewed a pan of coffee and chicory root. He'd motion at his latest stamps: gem-coloured beetles, vivid birds from the tropics. Sometimes, he'd have a new pigeon stamp affixed in a separate folder alongside sepia photographs of his prize racers. We'd walk out back to the pigeon loft, him talking as much to the birds as to me. He'd hand me a prize flyer, show me how to wait until she was comfortable, how to feel the way her talons gripped differently, wariness relaxing into curiosity. Then he'd show me how to stroke her neck with the back of a forefinger, how to smooth over her wings with the open palm of a whole hand. He'd roll cooing sounds around his throat, explain the differences between "flyers" and "fanciers"—one bred for flight, the other for show. He said some colombophiles even bred utility birds for butchery, but he couldn't butcher one of his birds. He explained types of flyers: the Birmingham Roller, the Tumbler—both known for their ability to somersault backward in midflight. And then his favourite: the Tippler, so called for its butterfly wing movement. A bird of long flight, up to twenty or so hours at times. You don't race Tipplers, or wait for them to return home. Tipplers, you simply release into the air, watch them circle alongside the other competitors' birds. And you wait, wait to see which bird lasts the longest airborne. A well-trained Tippler will descend upon its keeper's call. So, you have to be observant, follow your bird amongst the flock, know its wing pattern and whether it's tiring. Know when to call it down, when to let it coast. He told me Tipplers were bred from rock pigeons in nineteenth-century Britain. He wanted to visit Macclesfield to see where.

Once, sat on the yard step, a bird pecking at his greasy cardigan sleeves, Jean-Marie described the beginning of an event: the rise of the birds, dozens and dozens of bodies into air. The lightness, the precise movement, even the friction and flutter as they fought for clear space. He enjoyed the mass of them, knowing they'd fan out, knowing each carried within it the call of a different home, the sound of a different owner's voice. He said that was his favourite sight: birds leaving the ground, soaring God knows where.

*

Towards evening, I'd get ready for the night shift, rebandage my foot, and cycle the half hour to Mont Noir. I'd transfer ice cream from the churners into tubs. I'd cart the jambonneaux from one shelf to another, the saucisses and biftecks, the côtelettes d'agneau, scour stainless steel. I'd try to avoid going too frequently for a piss, though it was impossible with the cold, and the warm water, which you needed so your fingers could keep working, could sort through dead meat.

*

I only lived in Bailleul a few months. Midwinter to spring. Irregular work. Irregular pay. A house not mine. A bed not mine. A bike not mine. A life, in a way, not my own. Strange holding space. It was the kind of place into which one drifts, without fully understanding how, and from which one increasingly sees no exit. A swallowing kind of small town.

I had just started a relationship that would see me ignore my sexuality for another three years. My gender would have to wait another seven. It's possibly why I liked the region so much: it offered the gift of deferral, of loss.

I had left home, hadn't yet started university, was adrift. I did not know that I would get much lonelier, much more leaden in how I spoke and acted. How I'd hate where I lived, what I did. Did not know that my OCD would, ironically, get out of control, that I'd start working thirteen-hour days, go a week at a time without talking so that when I thanked a cashier, my voice cracked—broken, dust-choked thing. That I'd punch a wall when, once, I slept past 5:00 a.m. and lost two hours work time. That I'd have to pack the knuckles with ice for three days. That, even further down the line, I'd struggle to work, would spend hours lying in bed, letting food and wrappers and crockery fall over the covers, that I'd go all day, watch the sun rise, burn, set. That I'd tear my shoulder muscles, fall ill, that my mind would falter, everything—limbs, organs, thoughts—would grind to a standstill. That I'd get into bed, and rise months later—unsteadily at that. That people I didn't think would die, would. That some would do me kindness, others—harm. And I, likewise. Back then, I did not know how my life would collide.

Yet, looking now at this body stood in front of the abbey, I'm not sure if I'd have any advice for myself. Other than the soft promise that events would shift, that water would carry, would wash me somewhere unexpected—whether smooth or shattered. That there would always be quiet touchstones, every day, flecks of lapis in the bedrock. Like the abbey. And Jean-Marie, how he whispered round a kitchen, how the day breathed a little easier in talk with him. Or the tumble of birds in flight. And how, with time, a body will cast it all in different light: lost, resurfacing— phosphorescence splintering the night.

*

Eventually, seeing me limp too long, Jean-Marie visited me one morning: "Ça suffit, you work this morning? Non? Bien. We're going to see someone who can help with the foot."

In his right hand, he carried a small hutch, a pair of fantails pecking at the loose sawdust: "There's a breeder, near the abbey, known for fighting cocks and guard dogs. He's healed people in the past. It's not talked of openly, but my aunt, she saw him once, after her husband passed. She was left with two children to raise and a rash that broke around her mouth. Doctors couldn't help. He did." I leant more heavily on the door handle as Jean-Marie talked, lifting my right foot off the linoleum. Jean-Marie noticed, waved downwards: "Ah, tu vois, this is what I mean, this foot of yours." Shaking his head slightly, he continued, "Anyway, I spoke with him. Because, despite his talents, he can only breed fighting things. Animals that maul, break skin. Each their own gift. So, we struck a deal. I bring him a different kind of beast," Jean-Marie gestured to the fantails, "and he will look at your foot for me."

*

The breeder cut a slice of honeycomb, slid it from the knife into his tea as he watched the fantails strut across the kitchen table.

"Wonderlik." The breeder regularly traded across the Low Countries, spoke French, Dutch, German, and English. But Flemish was his mother tongue, and it was in Flemish that he spoke with Jean-Marie, whose own mother had come from Ghent, Belgium.

Sipping my tea, I watched the fantails. Not far off, an electric heater whined, sporadically clicked. The smell of charred dust settled acrid over the furniture. Taking my hands from my teacup, I rubbed a cramp in my calf. One of the fantails fluttered to where plates dried on a striped rag, tried to perch upon a glass only to clutch the sink edge, where it shat against the ceramic. The breeder smiled at the bird as he crushed a cardamom pod against the table with the flat of his knife, stirring it into the tea with the honey. I shifted in my seat to move nearer the heater. For the first time, the breeder looked over at me: "So," he tapped his knife against the rim of the china cup, "you are here for a foot?"

I lay on a rattan divan in the corner, its legs splinted and bound to keep it upright. The breeder removed my shoes and socks, told Jean-Marie that I mustn't wear them again. I was to burn them with fresh-cut rosemary and rinse the ashes from the ground with milk.

As Jean-Marie smoothed one of the fantails' bills with his thumb, the breeder washed my foot in a pewter basin. I remember my surprise at how delicately he held my foot, how he rested it on his knee, cupped the water so that it fell rhythmically over the torn skin. After months of doctors and nurses handling my foot for injections and incisions, craning to examine the sole as they bent it back, I'd grown jittery, developed a slight tremor in the leg. But, lying there, I relaxed, my shoulder blades sinking into the stained cushions of the divan. The breeder rubbed the skin with cedar oil, and applied a gritty paste. Having wound the foot in muslin, he placed two drops of spruce oil under my tongue.

The breeder walked into another room, returned with a pair of socks darned at both heels: "For now." As I pulled on the ill-fitting socks, wondering if they had ever been cleaner than my own, the breeder sat back at the table, flicked through a calendar, and marked the date of the next full moon. Rising hesitantly, I limped over to Jean-Marie, the poultice already silting uncomfortably between my toes. The breeder explained to Jean-Marie how I was not to remove the dressing until that date, but how, on that night, I was to rinse the foot in wild water without looking at the sole. I wasn't to look at the foot, not then, not thereafter. Not think of it either. I was to push it from eyes and mind, until much, much later: one day I would look by accident—"and then you will see."

As I made to leave, the breeder reached across the table to a chipped faïence bowl and removed half an orange from under a piece of bone lace. Flies lifted, resettled. "It was a late change, by the fates," the breeder cut a wedge from the orange, "seeing you born under the Ram and not the Fishes."

I hadn't told Jean-Marie or the breeder my date of birth, nor how my mother, due to deliver in early March, had groaned through most of the month. How, once induced, she held off to avoid a day darkened by family history—a feat that shunted my birth date from Pisces to Aries, from water to flame. Nor had I told him how, when I was born, my skin flaked from my body as if scorched, how the midwife called it a baptism of fire. My body a hot red thing of openings, convulsing with the world.

The breeder bit the orange up to the peel, chewed: "And by only a couple of days at that. Anyhow, even if you have been born to hooves and hide, you're to swim towards the Fishes, water, you must move towards water."

I watched the breeder suck the orange peel, each thumb, watched him wipe them on his shirt front: "Seems counterintuitive: have me born late only to spend my life going back."

"Well, that's the prerogative of the gods—to demand beyond the earth. Besides, you're to die many times in this life. The asteroid had to usher you in."

*

A fortnight later, I took a night train to Dunkirk, disembarked under the shivering light of a winter full moon. Flemish buildings—narrow, ornate—jutted at varying heights, jostled beside postwar concrete. The beach yawned empty. Wind bit brine. I limped to the shoreline, dropped my duffel on the damp sand, tugged off the Hi-Tec Squash Classics I'd bought cheap at the market, and stuffed my gym socks inside. I wore jeans, two T-shirts, a sweatshirt, scarf, windbreaker, and gloves. I shuddered from the cold anyway. Rolling my jeans to the knee, I unwound the bandage—greasy, foul-smelling. Rotten thing. After two weeks of waiting, I walked into the surge and swell of the North Sea, into a body cold enough to rid me, even briefly, of my own limbs.

Stood on that beach, my feet submerged, I watched the water bruise blue-black, foam white in the moonlight. Stood in the bright ring of iron-cold water, I let the tide take me in and out. I thought of the breeder: his easy-iron shirt and trousers, both stained, the trousers held up by a length of frayed nylon rope. How I'd tried not to stare at it, at the house in general, the way amputated car parts covered the floor, how agricultural tools—callipers, clippers, punches—glinted between the knives and forks. How I couldn't tell the carpet pattern from tracked-in mud. Yet in the midst of that, the grace, the precision with which the breeder stirred tea, applied unguent. Jean-Marie always referred to him as the breeder, never the healer. I wanted to know: How does one come to either profession? How do you acknowledge a gift for breeding and healing ferocity?

Most of all, though, I replayed what the breeder had said about my birth. Tried not to think how he knew that. It made me somewhat uneasy, similar to when Jean-Marie drove us up the winding trail to the house, drove us past cages of fighting cockerels—sudden ricochet of feather, claw, beak. The inexplicability. The intimacy. There was nothing malicious in what the breeder had said, and, yet, I felt it as threatening somehow—as a panting, muzzled thing at my back: *It was a late change, by the fates, seeing you born under the Ram and not the Fishes. Besides, you're to die many times in this life. The asteroid had to usher you in.*

*

When the nurses informed my mother that she was to be induced for a March 22 birth, she refused. "We can't have another man born on that day." Both my maternal great-grandfathers—men born to the trailing smoke of the Victorian industrial era, to colonial empire, world war, to steam trains, telegrams, and the first whine of public radio—both these men shared aggressive temperaments, a certain disdain for women, and March 22 birthdays. Even my mother's sister, seeing that the nurses clearly thought this a trivial case of prenatal histrionics, turned from the bedside: "No, really, we can't have any births on the twenty-second."

Why prenatal "histrionics," or superstition, or familial history, aren't valid reasons for a mother to decide her own induction date, I don't know. Maybe because the nurses, unlike my mother—who refused to be told my gender and believed she was carrying a boy—knew she'd be having a girl. Then again, maybe my mother's intuition was right.

The nurses kept their word. And their date. My mother kept hers. I was born late into the night of March 23, eight pounds, twelve ounces, partially deaf and burnt all over.

*

Three months after that night on the beach in Dunkirk, after the water took me in and out, thoughts swirling at depth, I caught a train to Ghent. Towelling myself down in a cheap motel bathroom, I caught sight of my soles. The skin had healed without a single scar.

*

Last year, the memory of the breeder resurfaced—wet, unsteady. I thought of Jean-Marie again, how, when he sat on the yard step that one time, he told me living got better with age. And even now, my grandmother always maintains that she is the happiest she has

ever been at eighty-five. How my mother, my aunt—how everyone
I know understands themselves better later in life. How my mother,
water rippling over her body in the bath, declares that she'd never
be in her twenties again, or thirties, that age brings an expanse, the
years a breadth. To break, repeatedly. To grow accustomed to that. .
The body—a slippery vessel. Tectonic thing, all collision and shattering impact. Then sudden smooth surface.

*

People have asked me since if I thought it would work, if I thought
what I was doing was mad, considered the breeder a fraud, Jean-
Marie a dupe. The truth is that I wasn't thinking, at least not in any
worded, well-ordered way. I never argued out the logic or illogic in
seeing the breeder, in catching a night train to rinse God-knows-
what from my foot under a full moon. It didn't feel all that strange,
or, rather, it didn't feel out of keeping with a world that bent beyond
clear understanding. I'm also persuaded that there comes a point
with pain, illness, bodily fatigue, when one simply does not care
anymore, when one's cultural norms or pride, one's arrogance, fear,
or whatever it is that keeps us thinking certain things will work and
others not, that maintains a "normal" and a "logical"—it falters. Or at
least it did for me. I did not know if it would work. I thought, scep-
tically, that it probably wouldn't, but it was worth a go. What did
I have to lose? And I trusted Jean-Marie: I believed what he said
about his aunt. I wanted to try for him, out of respect, out of thanks.
And even then, all things aside, what was so bad about any of this?
I remember thinking—alone on the beach, salt-heavy air rolling off
the dark water—that if nothing else, those events had brought me to
a moment worth standing in.

*

And the Fish in the River Shall Die

"The third angel poured his bowl into the rivers and the springs of water, and they became blood."
>—The Book of Revelation 16:4, New Revised Standard Version

A chain of shallow lagoons west of the Azov Sea, the Сиваш, or Syvash, is informally referred to as the "Putrid" or "Rotten Sea"—Гнилое Море in Russian, Гниле Море in Ukrainian, Чюрюк Денъиз in Crimean Tatar.

In November 1920, the final battle of the Russian Civil War was fought in the shallows of the Syvash. In a surprise attack, the Red Army marched through its waters, overwhelmed the White Army, and ended the Civil War in the largest massacre of its history, which is to say in a bloodbath of fifty thousand men. Almost a century later, Russia illegally annexed the Crimea from a newly independent

Ukraine, and the Syvash once more found itself a site of acute territorial conflict.

Although the sea's official name, Сиваш, comes from the Russian and Ukrainian root сив—meaning grey or ashen—and its Crimean Tatar appellation, Сываш, means "dirt," the Syvash's waters have the distinctive quality of being neither grey, nor muddied. Instead, they shift from pink to bright, blood red.

Who knows where the bowl fell—red water, Red Army, bloodshed.

The Georgian Military Road

The last time I spoke Russian had been years before, in 2012, when
I took Russian classes in Perm, a settlement located in the western foothills of the Ural Mountains. A Soviet closed city and driving force in the aeronautics and armaments industries, Perm only
began appearing on maps in the 1990s, around the same time officials changed its name from Molotov and stopped referring to it
as "Gateway to the Gulag." In Perm, I took lodgings in an apartment owned by a retired schoolteacher. Widowed, with two grown
sons, Tatiana Ivanovna was a heavyset woman who wore gingham
nighties and bright slippers that I learnt to call тапочки; who swore
by two slices of mutton fat for breakfast and a thin noodle soup for
lunch; who kept foot-high jars of salted gherkins on the balcony;
who liked fermented milk, cats, and figurines of dancing balleri-
nas and Cossacks; who knew the daytime TV schedule by rote, and
read romance paperbacks, stopping only to click on the radio at

11:00 p.m. for *Сердце Говорит*—*The Heart Speaks*—when female callers aired their romantic dilemmas to the show's psychologist host, a man who invariably advised them to listen to their husbands, try harder with their makeup, or buy new stockings.

The last time I spoke Russian, I sat watching television with Tatiana Ivanovna, the bulky set wavering blue-white over the china statuettes. An effeminate male presenter hosted an American talk show dubbed into Russian. Tatiana readjusted the tasselled cushions: "Why is there so much homosexuality in America, when that illness doesn't exist in Russia?"

The last time I spoke Russian, I listened as the men who drove me and a friend home talked about faggots—that if they saw a faggot, they'd beat that man, for their wives, for their children, they'd remove that piece of shit from the ground.

The last time I spoke Russian, I met a masculine-presenting photographer, a woman hired because she was well connected, good at her job. A woman who worked quietly, always asked gently that someone change pose, shift places. A woman who invited her employers to an exhibition of her work—men who handed her a drink, talked of photography, then joked out of earshot: *She must fuck dogs, looking like that.*

The last time I spoke Russian, I shared dinner with a closeted gay man who, at forty-nine, slept with a gun at his bedside, who admitted to waking in sweats, to vomiting, to having put himself in a bathtub one night after almost being found having sex with another man, who let himself shake and vomit and piss and shit until he could deal with it, until he could clean the bath, could rinse his body from itself.

The last time I spoke Russian, I was in a relationship with a man. I presented as female, passed for cisgender and heterosexual. In one of the world's most homophobic countries, my sexuality, always snarling to the side of me, finally caught up. Bit into this body until it showed itself, raw, bloodied. I left Russia single.

It would take another three years for me to come to terms with my gender.

Some six years after living in Perm, I would take a trip to Georgia—the first time I would return to Eastern Europe as openly queer and transmasculine.

*

The Georgian Military Road gradually evolved from dirt path to horse track as travellers, silk route traders, and invaders wound their way between Tbilisi, Georgia, and Vladikavkaz, Russia.

The mountain pass first appeared in the writings of Strabo and Pliny the Elder, reappearing millennia later in the diaries of Mikhail Lermontov. It eventually found its way into the travel literature of *Baedeker's Russia 1914*, the guide insisting the route's beauty warranted its ten-hour journey time.

Imperial Russian troops traversed the pass in 1769 in a military effort that would see Georgia shift from Persian to Russian rule. Not long after, the Russian soldier, statesman, and writer Count Pavel Sergeevich Potemkin sent eight hundred men to work on the road so that, by the autumn of 1783, he was able to ride in an eight-horse carriage to Tiflis—the city that would become modern-day Tbilisi. Construction of the Georgian Military Road continued long into the nineteenth and twentieth centuries, the project taken up by the Soviet Union after the fall of the Russian Empire.

The road remains a vein of political interaction between Georgia and Russia. In 2006, Russia closed its border at the mountain pass checkpoint in a gesture of support for the Georgian breakaway territories, Abkhazia and South Ossetia. The political tension escalated into military conflict in 2008. The border remained closed until 2010, when Armenia pressed for a reopening, its economy suffering from lack of automotive trade route.

*

Tbilisi, Georgia, 2018: Ivano owned a mechanic shop in Tbilisi, drove tourists at the weekend to make some extra cash. I was in Tbilisi for three weeks, to help run a literary seminar. An acquaintance had given me Ivano's number, insisting I visit the Gergeti Trinity Church in Stepantsminda, Kazbegi, before I left Georgia.

That morning, the light still pale as it crushed pink over the city, Ivano met me on Tbilisi's Liberty Square. Normally four lanes deep in growling traffic, the square was deserted. A white Mercedes Sprinter tore across three lanes, swerved onto the sidewalk. The door swung open, my name ringing across the tarmac: "Lars?"

Driving through the city, Ivano and I followed the motorway along the Mtkvari River—a wide, muddied channel, where men fished, flasks of coffee beside wire keep baskets, a trout or two already slapping against the pavement.

"I was a saxophonist, played in the Georgian Symphony Orchestra. А сейчас, now, I drive tourists. I like the people, talking to people from elsewhere."

I turned my attention from the river to Ivano, blinking from the sunlight. Ivano rummaged in the van door, handed me a faded ball cap: "I had a student once, talented boy. Even gave him my saxophone when I retired. I remember the day—hot, late autumn. He came for his lesson, and I thought, *This is it, Ivano, today.* And so, I did. At the end of the hour, I gave him the sax. Вот. He never went on with it. Got drunk, lost it in a taxi. Three generations of musicians, craftmanship—left in a taxi. Well, so be it."

I turned the ball cap in my hands before putting it on, the cotton soft, the red an almost coral colour from years of sun. It reminded me of a T-shirt my father used to wear to the beach in summertime—an oversized, salt-stained thing that always looked ill-fitting on a man who, born in 1937, never wore anything besides button-downs and brogues. Even at the beach, he wore leather shoes. The T-shirt was his concession to being in the 1990s; that and going sockless in the leather lace-ups.

"We spoke not long ago. He's in construction—told me how he should've tried out for the conservatory like I said. I remember his hands—wrecked from lifting, from metal, bricks, cement. I asked if he still played. He doesn't."

I tried to imagine this boy, to not think of my father, whose body, in his eighties, was more fragile than I'd ever seen it. Ivano glanced at me sideways, "You're British, yes? My sons speak English. Everyone under thirty speaks English; everyone over thirty speaks Russian. Of course, no one wants to speak Russian anymore, not after seventy years of Soviet occupation."

So far, in Tbilisi, not knowing enough Georgian, I'd predominantly spoken English. On occasion, I'd spoken Russian, but only a few basic phrases—foodstuffs, directions—and only when there was no other common language.

*

After the 1917 Russian Revolution, Georgia broke away from Imperial Russia, officially establishing its independence on May 26, 1918, a sovereignty supposedly recognised by Russia in the 1920 Treaty of Moscow. Yet in 1921, a mere four years after emerging from imperial rule, Georgia was once again invaded, only this time by Soviet forces mobilised under the pretext of supporting the Georgian "peasants and workers." Russian forces took the Georgian capital on February 25, 1921, in an assault that resulted in mass casualties and the fall of the nation within the following three weeks.

A little over a month later, the National Georgian Government—overthrown and exiled to Istanbul—called upon the international community for aid. The plea was met with silence. Three years later, in the summer of 1924, the Georgian people rebelled against Bolshevik rule. In response, the Soviet security officer Lavrentiy Beria mounted mass repressions that would see, within a single week, up to 10,000 people executed and 20,000 exiled to Siberia. The reprisals would also see the submission of the Georgian state, the country relegated to a tourist destination for top-ranking Soviet officials for the next five decades.

*

"You understand Russian better than you suggest, I see it." Ivano faced me as we idled at an intersection. "You followed what I said about the saxophone. This is good. I don't speak English; you don't speak Georgian, so, давай, we'll speak Russian."

I had learnt Russian as an undergraduate. Save for the few words I'd exchanged over market stalls in the past couple of weeks, I hadn't read or spoken a word since. I had no desire to speak Russian in Georgia, a country for which Russian had consistently accompanied cultural repression and violence. Besides, I was uncomfortable speaking Russian. It reminded me of people and places that I tended to keep at a distance, that surfaced during baths taken in the early hours, the body dissolving, memories smearing the tile. The images of myself—the most difficult to wipe clean: "I don't speak Russian anymore, Ivano. Once, yes. А сейчас, нет."

A church slipped by in the distance. Ivano took his hand from the gearstick and pressed his fingertips to a cloth icon dangling from the rearview mirror. For a moment, the seven swords piercing Virgin Mary Softener of Evil Hearts were eclipsed, but just as quickly his hand fell back, put the van into fifth: "Не важно, you understand. Besides, a language should never be lost. I tell my sons, all languages are worth speaking, even Russian. So, I speak Russian. We will speak Russian. Давай, разговаривай со мной!"

I turned to look out the window again as Ivano emptied his shirt pocket onto the dashboard—flip phone, Biro, crushed packet of Dunhill King Size. Outside, the river grew wider, the sides steeper. Houses clung to the rock face; rooms somehow suspended above a fifty-foot drop.

I ran my hand over the cotton of the ball cap, felt the air leave my lungs, my body slacken into the five-hour ride. I turned to Ivano, motioning to the fish in the keep baskets along the bank: "Какие рыбы ловятся здесь?"

"You don't speak Russian, but you'll learn the names of fishes?"

∗

Saint Petersburg, Russia, 2010: "Окунь, хариус, щука." *Perch, grayling, pike.* Feodor poured more tea into his teacup. He always brewed tea in a small pot, letting it sit until it carried a bitter tannin sheen. After that, he'd boil water when he wanted tea, add it to half a cup of the tarry mixture from the pot. "Угорь." *Eel.* Feodor took a shrivelled lemon from the fridge, cut a slice for my cup, then his. I sat at the breakfast table, slowly sifting through the photographs he'd brought from the room he shared with his wife. I only once saw inside that room—a sliver of dark wood wardrobe, the mirror water-damaged, a patina of black stains blooming at the edge.

Feodor and Natalia had left Tomsk for Saint Petersburg when Feodor, once a miner, had contracted TB, his lungs already weak from years of dust and grit. Now, he spent his days in the flat's bedroom, sitting on the balcony, watching daytime TV. They rented out the second room in their apartment to help pay his medical bills, which is how I came to know them. Enrolled in a beginner's Russian program, the summer after my first year at university, I rented the room in their bitten-up apartment, roads rumbling eleven floors down, June heat slamming off asphalt.

Feodor lifted a four-pint Kilner jar from the floor, unscrewed the lid that rusted tight every time he replaced it, and stirred варенье, a homemade blackcurrant jam, into each of our cups. He sat, looked at the faded print in my hands: Feodor—younger, muscular—stood alongside a river in ditched red shorts and dirty ball cap. A fish hung from his hand. Behind him, the water coursed under razored sunlight. Sipping his tea, Feodor gestured at the print: "Налим." *Burbot.*

I shuffled the photographs: a teenager reclined on a threadbare sofa, a Kazakhstani rug covering the wall. The boy, half smiling, half frowning, braced a gun across his chest. "Сын." *Son.*

*

The motorway yawned asphalt, ochre dust. Wastelands coughed car wrecks, plastic trash. Neon bled into daylight—a red haze that whispered over Ivano's body as he walked between the gas station pumps, returned carrying extra cigarettes, coffee in paper cups.

On the roadside, men hawked watermelons out of beaten-up Ladas. For the most part, the men sat in fold-out chairs under the sparse shade of taped-up parasols. Occasionally, a vendor sliced a watermelon on a crate, walked over to another, shared the fruit.

Lighting a cigarette, Ivano looked sideways at me: "Ну скажи, why did you stop speaking Russian?"

*

Ivano and I drove until tarmac gave way to dirt track, until the hawkers disappeared from sight. We drove until concrete fell away to fig trees. Until vines smothered outhouses in thick-stemmed green. Until men and women carried rolls of wire and wooden-handled tools, shouldered sacks of potatoes across bare backs. One village spat torn tyres, rusted engines. In another, painted wooden signs flanked the roadside: ხინკალი. ХИНКАЛИ. *KHINKALI.* Where exactly anyone might actually buy the khinkali, or dumplings, was hard to tell; there were few doors, and all were bolted, hidden in honeysuckle.

We drove until the lushness of villages gave out, or rather gave over—engulfed. Mountains rose and fell—some great muzzle breathing mist. The road narrowed and widened by turns, sometimes asphalt, other times a loose shingle pitted with potholes.

Fog hung low that day, rolled down ravines with dull weight.

Falcons circled. I remember the strangeness of that place, cars, people—all of us irrelevant, dissolving into landscape. The ricochet of streams, the sudden silence as one raced over a rock shelf—cold, clear, slicing—how it smashed against granite. And the storms: how the windscreen wipers swept at the driving rain, the view momentarily gleaming, luminous, before it drowned again, submerged under a falling firmament.

Ivano shifted in his seat. "You know, in Georgia," Ivano pointed downwards, presumably at Georgia in general, but landing more at the van's gearstick, "we call the Georgian-Russian border crossing the Kazbegi Checkpoint, but in Russia, they call it the Верхний Ларс." In English, Верхний Ларс translates to the "Upper Lars." Ivano looked over at me, his torso straining the seat belt: "So, tell me, how does it feel to be a line between mountains?"

*

In 2012, after completing my studies, I left Perm. In 2013, Vladimir Putin signed Article 6.21 of the Code of Administrative Offenses of the Russian Federation, a law that prohibits distributing information amongst minors of "non-traditional sexual relations." Individuals engaging in such "propaganda" can be fined or jailed. In a report issued in 2014 by the United Nations Committee on the Rights of the Child, the law was deemed to encourage "the stigmatization of and discrimination against lesbian, gay, bisexual, transgender and intersex (LGBTI) persons, including children, and children from LGBTI families." The committee recommended the law be repealed. The law still stands.

Volgograd, Russia, May 9, 2013: The morning after the anniversary of World War II Victory Day, the city still listless after the previous day's parades, the body of twenty-three-year-old Vladislav Tornovoi is discovered abandoned in a courtyard. Raped with broken beer bottles. Genitals mutilated. Skull smashed by rocks. In a video released online, one of the three suspects answers questions as to why they attacked Tornovoi: "Because he said he was gay." In statements to the police and media, Tornovoi's family and friends respond to the murder with a single message: "He wasn't gay."

Zaporozhye, Kamchatka Peninsula, Russia, May 28, 2013: The thirty-eight-year-old deputy director of Petropavlovsk-Kamchatsky airport, Oleg Serdyuk, is beaten, stabbed to death, and driven into the forest, his body doused with gasoline and left to burn through the night. Three suspects are tried and sentenced to imprisonment at labour camps for terms of nine to twelve and a half years on the grounds of homophobic hate crime. The crime receives almost no news coverage: a single paragraph in two news outlets, and a short report for the *Echo of Moscow* stating that the event did not elicit any extraordinary interest among the region's inhabitants.

December 29, 2014: The Russian government passes a road safety law that denies individuals driving licenses should they possess certain "mental and behavioural disorders": *schizophrenia, schizotypal and delusional disorders, dissociative personality disorders, dual-role transvestism, transsexualism.*

April 1, 2017: The *Novaya Gazeta* newspaper publishes reports of a state-led concentration camp in Argun, Chechnya, revealing that over a hundred men have been abducted, imprisoned, and tortured on grounds of homosexuality. The article's sources, which include members of the Chechen Special Forces, confirm at least three extrajudicial deaths at the camp with many more suspected. The Chechen government claims the article is an April fool's joke: There are no homosexuals in Chechnya; if there were, the Special Forces wouldn't have to respond—their families would kill them instead.

December 2018: More than a year later. The Organization for Security and Co-operation in Europe (OSCE) confirms that persecution of LGBT persons did take place in Chechnya and was ignored by authorities.

December 2018–January 2019: Another wave of "forced disappearances" spreads across Chechnya. The Russian LGBT Network estimates forty persons detained, two killed.

*

A monk's burial site, its earth said to secrete holy oil. The fresco of a baptism, in which yellow fishes nibbled on a man's legs—fish with wide, forked fins and elongated bodies, strange beasts shimmering somewhere between minnows and catfish. A church whose architect, having watched its final stone be placed, severed his own hand so he could never build a more beautiful edifice. At each of these places, Ivano pulled over, gestured beyond the windscreen, "Go, look." Deeper into the mountains, Ivano drove us around donkeys, saddlebags laden with grapes, between women sat on patterned rugs, selling fruit by the fistful. I rolled down the window, mist swallowing my forearm, parts of my face. An old man leant on a cane, bundles of churchkhela heaped over each shoulder, his body softened under multicoloured weight. A church stood some way off. I jumped down from the passenger cabin, red dust clouding at my feet.

Inside the church, jewellery hung from an icon of the Weeping Virgin: rosaries, figaro chains, bloodstone-set rings. A monk asked me if I wished to make an offering to the Virgin, said that leaving an item worn against skin was best, that the soul carried in the body's heat. I looked at my wrists. The only jewellery I had was a beat-up Casio. I wasn't sure the Virgin was really in the market for digital watches, even if they did have a date-adjust backlit display. Undoing the Casio, I rubbed the strap against my T-shirt. My body was an uncomfortable mix of dampness and dust. At my Catholic secondary school, we had always been taught that one gave Our Lady a burden one wished to shed. On reflexion, the Georgian Virgin was running a much better racket. Apologising to the icon, I took a coin from my pocket, prayed she'd chalk it up to cultural difference, that she'd wash the memory corroding my throat and lips.

*

Earlier that week in Tbilisi, I took a cab to an Olympic lido at the city's outskirts. The driver, Giorgi, hit the gas and the brake with equal weight, cut fast across lanes, pausing only to cross himself as we passed a church, after which he resumed swearing at other cars, lit a cigarette, and crossed himself again as he undertook a truck.

Slipstreaming through traffic in that '90s Corolla sedan, I watched through the cracked windscreen as scarred tower blocks emerged from the muggy heat. Men hawked flip-flops, rubber footballs, packets of roasted nuts. We drove past a dumping ground, gutted ice cream refrigerators leaning blue-green-pink beside seatless truck cabins.

Built for the 2015 European Youth Summer Olympic Festival, the outdoor pool rose out of a wasteland—concrete, geometric—the façade peeling poster-block red. Giorgi explained how, after the games, the pool stood abandoned, the water dirtying. Eventually, the city council made it public. "People come on their days off," Giorgi told me, "they drive out here and they rest." He said he liked to drive out here, swim a stretch.

I stood for a moment in the dust and heat. In the distance, a crane lifted a Ford Escort until it was high above the rubble of car parts, until the sun gleamed off the chassis. For a moment, the car hung there, swayed slightly on the chain jib—tyreless, windowless, trunk gaping. Then the claw tightened: papery movement of hydraulics, metal, glass.

Not long out of a relationship, unemployed, and living back with my mother, I came to Tbilisi unable to sleep. That morning, I lay awake from 4:00 a.m., the radio's low murmur settling over my skin.

As I exited the changing rooms, cold tile ceding to hot concrete, I hoped Giorgi was right, that this place could wash a person from themself. I skirted the whitewashed diving tower, wove between sun loungers and scattered Coke cans. The Olympic pool glittered beneath the stands. I stepped onto the starting block, took my mark, tensed. I shot into a blue so electric it stung. For two hours, I relinquished to sunlight shafting through water, to the digital pace clock. Blue to swallow a body. Blue to dissolve weight, the heaviness of blood and days.

Afterwards, I lay on a plastic lounger, sank into a heavy static of cigarettes and sunscreen, polyester and sweat. Russian pop music drifted from a PA system. Bathers crashed through the water, re-emerged seconds later to flop across towels, chatting as they swigged warm beer. In the distance, far beyond the pool deck, beyond the dumping ground, the city outskirts, beyond the Ford Escort that, by now, was likely a block of splintered metal, the beginnings of the Caucasus mountain chain wrapped around the horizon—colossal, slumbering, immobile. And, for a moment, lying exhausted against white plastic, I felt my chest breathe open, felt this body unfold. As if held somehow, in heat and colour, in a slowness of soft hours.

In the changing rooms, I walked to my locker, towelled myself. A woman who had been undressing beside my locker looked at me, walked off. She returned with a dozen women and a couple of young girls. Flip-flops slapped against the tiling, stopped at my back. I paused, arm reaching into the locker. I measured one deep breath. Looking downward to avoid anyone's gaze, I turned from the locker. The women circled me. I took in the fourteen pairs of flip-flops—lime green, neon pink, glittery pompoms. The women stared, arms folded, each fully dressed. One woman chewed gum; another clicked her tongue. The young girls, only twelve or thirteen, didn't say a word. A woman shifted her weight. I turned back to the locker, thought of my mother—hours, years of her care. Staring into the locker, the women still at my back, I took the towel from my shoulders. *That I be kept safe. That a mother's attentions not spill across tile.* I passed the towel over my chest, stomach, legs.

Memories jarred. A child pointing at me as I shower: "What is it?" The mother: "It's a woman; there are lady parts." Two teenage girls, their clothed bodies slamming me, half-undressed, against a wall: "What the fuck are you?" At a new job: "Is it a man or a woman?" And the answer from someone who has asked me once to pass the salt at lunch: "She's a woman."

"But is she a woman who wants to be a man?"

"No."

"But she's more man than woman, no?"

What is it? What the fuck are you? Man or woman? Always: my body silent, strangely preferring the questions to their answers. Even when violent.

The women watched me dry off, apply deodorant, dress. Pulling my swim gear from the locker, I stuffed it into my bag and turned around again. For the first time in those long few minutes, I moved my gaze from the women's feet to their faces. The woman chewing gum took it from her mouth and crushed it into an old receipt. The girls' mother placed her hands on their shoulders. The woman who had initially been changing next to me now stood directly opposite. She looked me up and down. We stared at one another, the changing room noiseless. Not a shower running, not a hair dryer blowing. No slack, sun-jaded talk. I waited until the woman unfolded her arms, moved aside to let me pass. Her blouse brushed my shoulder in cotton forget-me-nots. I said nothing as I walked down the corridor, nothing as I passed the reception desk, customer service, as I stepped through the glass doors and into the ochre heat. Outside, I called a taxi, watched the crane jib swing cars between far-off mountain peaks. The wasteland rippled in scorched grasses. All around me, cicadas screamed.

*

Ivano pulled off the road onto the hard shoulder—a narrow dirt strip that, two paces from the car, dropped away, cavernous. Ivano cut the engine, stepped out, lit a cigarette. To the side, an elderly man roasted corncobs over a rusted tin drum. "It's the mineral deposits." Ivano gestured at the valley below, where two rivers met— one milky, the other slate. Water exploded grey-white against rock. "That's what gives them the colour." Ivano flicked the ash off his cigarette: "People bring their difficulties to the rivers, speak them into the water. It's said they'll roll deep after that, carry in salts and silt and grit, that the rivers will take what you told them." Ivano stubbed out the cigarette: "But this is wild water—beautiful, magic, ruinous. Therein lies the risk: whatever you give to the rivers is theirs to do with as they wish."

Ivano ambled over to the corn vendor, who chatted as he tore a page from a magazine, rubbing lard over the paper before he wrapped it around a cob. I watched as water met other water, stared until it carried, dredged memories from my chest.

*

I knew Feodor as gaunt. His hair worn in a self-shaved buzz cut. An Orthodox cross visible through the holes of his T-shirt. At first, Feodor simply nodded when we met in the kitchen. But, after a few days, he sat down as I was writing up verb tables, and, gently pushing the workbook aside, placed a cup of tea and photographs in its place. For the next week or so, that was how it went: Feodor making tea, showing me pictures of his home, his mother, his son, where he fished. He told me about growing up in Ukraine, about when he decided, one warm night, insects chattering, to take the sleeper train all the way to Tomsk in search of work. How the train had whispered him in and out of landscape; how he stumbled into the wild of that place after murmuring hours of doubt; how he found Natalia—always that, the story always wound its way to the same end point.

Natalia worked double shifts on the metro, rose early, returned midafternoon, cooked, cleaned, then headed out again for the night shift. She never talked much, just: "Hello," "Food—top shelf of fridge." Depending on the time of day, she referred to the room I rented as a bedroom, living room, study, dining room. I've since done the same, when living in bedsits, cheap single rooms that miraculously start to multiply. She was similar with Feodor: a few words dealt quickly, sparsely. Yet her devotion—the quiet, physical presence. Each gesture so that Feodor might eat, might forgive himself for not working and simply rest. I only ever heard her relax after a night shift. Sat in the kitchen, she'd phone her friend, who also worked as a metro driver and lived in a block of flats opposite. Natalia would open the window, and talk with a speed and liveliness I didn't recognise, her words tumbling out one window and carrying through my own, wide open, onto the sleepless night.

*

After five hours of tailing eighteen-wheelers and flatbed trucks, Ivano and I arrived at Stepantsminda. Shops lined the dirt road, their windows clotted with faded advertisements. Women sat on upturned milk crates, smoking as they sold dishes of peaches, cherries, cloth-wrapped cheeses. Ivano pulled over near an industrial gas station, made a call. "You'll go with my friend to the church. It's too steep for my car. He's coming now. I'll wait here, then, when you return, you can tell me how it was, being with God on a mountaintop."

The Mitsubishi Delica jolted along the rutted track, Zurab jerking the steering wheel left-right-left. In front and behind, Delicas climbed the mountain. I remembered thinking how strange a pilgrimage: no walking, no votives, no offerings, just vans, foam spilling from torn seats. Zurab switched radio stations. *EUROPE—THE FINAL COUNTDOWN* scrolled across the digital display, the song throbbing from speakers backlit in LEDs.

At a small clearing, Zurab swung the car to a stop. "The Gergeti church is up there." Zurab nodded at the peak, stuffed a pack of Dunhill Lights into his shirt pocket: "I'll stay here. You'll need to take the path." Jumping down from the car, I followed a steady line of tourists up the dirt track. After a few minutes, the line slowed, huddled into a stone porch. As with the other holy sites along the way, signs at the church entrance indicated that women must cover their heads, arms, and legs. Baskets of shawls and skirts stood beneath them. Each time the choice: dress as female and negate myself or forego the shawl and negate this religion, this culture that might not recognise my body as indistinct, as something else. Each time,

I waited at the threshold, not knowing how to stop my body from being a thing of disrespect. As I hesitated, a monk pointed for the two women in front of me to take a shawl. At my turn, he waved me directly into the church.

Wind ached through the nave as monks milled between the tourists. Feeble sunlight pooled across flagstone. Candles alleviated the darkness, whispered over lapis, vermillion, hammered gilt. I followed a monk replacing tapers, his habit skimming tourists' Nike Airs and Reebok Classics. At the iconostasis, I stopped beneath a mural of cherubim beholding Christ, their winged faces suspended in azure granite. On the upper left, a haloed figure—small, pale, peeling red—watched over the nave. The inscription, written in the Asomtavruli alphabet, Georgia's oldest script, read: "Saint Nino, Mother of Georgia."

Ivano had described how, in the early 2000s, restorers discovered the fresco hidden under a thick coat of blue paint. Most likely applied by a Russian exarch, the gesture aimed to quash Georgian nationalism by covering a saint known, amongst other appellations, as "the Enlightener." Saint Nino brought literal and metaphorical light to Queen Nana and King Mirian III of Georgia. Struck blind for his lack of faith, King Mirian III was restored to sight after he pleaded with "Nino's God." I thought back to Ivano describing the recovered icon as we made the journey, his hands gesticulating, lifting off the steering wheel, "Imagine that!" The van veered. Ivano slapped the steering wheel: "A light-bearing saint plunged into darkness, left for decades behind pigment." Ivano crossed himself, then grinned: "You know, it's a good omen, Georgia bringing light to the Enlightener. Imagine, repaying the favour to a saint, that's priceless—we can do no wrong now."

"Excuse me," an American tourist tapped my shoulder. "You know, you need to wear a shawl. They're in the baskets at the front." I nodded. The woman smiled, began photographing the iconostasis on her phone. Making the sign of the cross, I turned from Saint

Nino, congratulated her on her reappearance, and walked outside onto a ledge that wrapped around the church. I zipped my coat against the cold, watched vultures crest through the mist. Fog slithered across the ground, around the church brickwork, blotted sky and earth, only to clear in a gust of wind and reveal the drop gaping inches from my feet. I shuddered, stepped back. Around me, visitors took selfies, shouted and pointed when the air thinned, cramming into sudden shots—smiles, peace signs, star jumps. Behind me, I could still hear the monks murmuring devotions on the altar step, could taste the frankincense. I turned from the ledge and began my descent to where Ivano waited, far below, in the mountain's mouth.

*

I drifted in and out of sleep that month, years ago, in Saint Petersburg, limbs caught within the city's White Nights. I remember the strangeness of those early hours, how bleached, night after night of long, dusty warmth, tower blocks rising into pearlescent sky. I would lie on the corduroy sofa bed, the sound of cars and people rolling through the open windows. I would listen to this slow tide, people walking, drinking, bodies smudging through the disjoint.

I asked myself during those hours what it was about Feodor, how I felt so comfortable next to a man with whom I could barely communicate. A man who knew nothing of me—where I was from, how I spoke when unhindered by a language barrier, what I thought about politics or religion. A man who, in a culture that favoured women waiting on men, would hush me to sit, go about the domestic task of making tea for us both, who shared family photos by the stack. A man who couldn't get more stereotypically masculine in his profession, how he dressed, and, yet, who spoke with such softness as to make the air feel close. Who always took time to listen to me, to perform small gestures that anchored me in a country I didn't know, amongst people I'd never met. He never once drew attention to everything that separated us—language, gender, age, culture, education—never made our nationalities feel like a rift. He hit upon the one thing we both had in common: fishes.

I asked myself the same with Ivano, more so, given that this time I no longer passed as cisgender and heterosexual. I sat next to him, my body most often mistaken for male in Georgia, and he didn't comment, didn't look perplexed. Not once did he make me feel anything other than safe in his company. Even if Ivano read me as female and heterosexual, even if he suggested I marry his son, he still at another point talked of countries that had beautiful wine and women, winking as if, for the briefest moment, his intuitive understanding of me overwhelmed his cultural one. Somehow, like Feodor, Ivano saw me, the pace and gesture of me. Even when what he was understanding came without cultural framework, he grasped it—understanding as physicality, as a texture between bodies, unspoken yet sensed.

I'd like to think that being seen doesn't always fit easy delineation—neither the who, nor the how. Feodor and Ivano—white, cisgender, heterosexual, from homophobic and transphobic countries—welcomed this self in a manner that allowed for its slipperiness, even if they didn't refer to me as nonbinary or queer. These men reminded me that, sometimes, a simple softness between bodies might rinse hard knowledge. That we can find the sediment of ourselves unsettled. Hear another breathing, and know, in that rise and fall of chest, that the days are reckless, that this world—sweeping, swallowing current—has washed us into unforeseen waters, strange confluence.

*

I thanked Zurab, paid what I owed, and left the Delica's pounding radio for the quiet of the gas station. Ivano stood beside the minivan as I approached, fine rain blurring his body, vaporous as his cigarette smoke. Dampness had set in: the ground now mud, the vendors' grapes and redcurrants glassy in their bowls. Ivano started the engine. The van's headlamps liquefied in the gathering night. At one point, we passed vendors selling honey. Huddled under broken parasols, they refilled the kerosene lamps that spluttered between the jars. The honey glowed golden to deep molasses, unearthly, as if emitting its own light. We passed a glut of lorries, oil tankers, and trucks parked near a roadside hut—drivers leant over plates of kharcho, chakapuli. Near a village, a young boy ran beside cattle, herded colossal angular beasts. Our headlights fell across muzzles, horns, flanks, caught on breath that billowed—slow, translucent—that engulfed.

*

Between late May and early July, the sun never dips below the horizon in Saint Petersburg. The nights never fully darken. Streetlamps stand blank. The brightest period is considered to fall between June 11 and July 2. Twenty-one days, 504 hours—narrow slice of pale, slipping light.

For a fortnight of the month I spent in Saint Petersburg, Feodor came into the kitchen each day, set down a different sheaf of photographs, made us tea. One day, Feodor moved to a sanatorium. I left Russia before he came back.

Nine years after meeting Feodor in Saint Petersburg, and several months after leaving Ivano in Tbilisi, I thought back to that early morning as Ivano and I followed the Mtkvari River's yawning current. How the fish thrashed in wire keepnets, the men taking slow drags on cigarettes. And I remembered Feodor, his silence, his slow pace, how he brought an expanse, shone with the greyness of light breaking over landscape.

That day, far from both Ivano and Feodor, I looked up the Mtkvari River and learnt that almost sixty species of fish inhabit its waters, the most common being loach, bleak, trout, and nase. Карпообразные. Уклейки. Форель. Подуст.

*

In the years since I left Russia, I've openly lived as queer and transmasculine. I'm more at ease with this body, better understand its strange weight.

Yet, when Ivano asked me when would I marry; when he suggested I meet his youngest son—a computer engineer, a good man, a kind man; when he gave me his number, invited me to eat with his family that Sunday, drink wine he had bought in Kakheti, see the Mercedes 450SL he was rebuilding in the workshop; when he saw me hesitate, him looking back to the steering wheel, apologetic, saying he didn't mean to offend, when the last thing he'd done was offend me; when he took the long route through the city so he could drop me where I was lodging, waited in traffic after hours of driving, men leaning out of gridlocked cars, calling to acquaintances: "Hey! We're getting pilaf. Come. Eat with us." When Ivano, sensing that more than the day had come to a close—a bond now severed, drifting—when Ivano held my gaze all the same: "Come back if you can." And even when I reached over and embraced that man, his shoulders straining against the seat belt, even after I kissed each of his cheeks, praying as I did that he would carry gently through this world, I could never simply say: "Ivano, I've never loved men like that. Ivano, my body doesn't fit like you think it does. I want to break bread with you, meet your sons, want to drive with you again, follow water. Only, not as someone I'm not." If I could have given myself to be seen. Had enough faith in the love of this man. But I didn't, couldn't.

When I got back to my rented apartment in Tbilisi, I showered, lay on the bed. Engines idled outside; the occasional motorbike tore through the street. A man hauled sacks of cherries through a doorway, the corners leaking crushed fruit. I decided to live someone else's Friday night. I dressed, walked to a Turkish restaurant, ordered pilaf. Families crowded around small tables; children lapped the room. A Barbie flew into a corner, later reappeared, thrust headfirst into a dish of rice. A mother scolded about dolls and floors and dirt, and that's not what rice is for, and what are you playing at, go play with the dog at the door.

I sat next to the window, the street a rush of lamplight, traffic, of endless unknowable bodies. Everywhere, passers-by emerged from alleyways, cars, buses, only to disappear again, trail the night with darker, drowning depth. I pushed the rice around with my fork. I thought about Ivano, why I'd not been able to drag myself to the surface. Fear? Prejudice? And, if so, on his part or mine? Because I was leaving soon anyhow? I hadn't trusted myself to that man, a man who had shown me only kindness, who released me somehow at the day's end. I let thoughts settle, metallic. And I hoped that something of myself might surpass the distance. That Ivano might think well of me. That, at some point, he'd remember these hours, bodies sharing themselves in small gestures: a cigarette, apricots bought at traffic lights, words rolled back and forth in mist. That this self might shimmer before returning to lightless abyss.

I wandered over the day, around Ivano, the cut of that man, the texture and weight. How seeing me tired on the way back, he turned the radio on low: "Rest now, save those words for someone else." How the landscape submerged, resurfaced, how my body blurred in and out of sleep. I remembered the sheet rain, Ivano slowing the minivan to a creep.

That night, a thunderstorm rang out, flooded the valley electric. Water sluiced off the mountainside, the road suddenly live, writhing river-like—baptismal, apocalyptic.

Last Night, Sturgeon Swam the Streets

LIV. Beasts—ancient, armoured—scattered the lamplight, settled beneath trucks, swept past shopfronts. Last night, I dreamt my soul was a sturgeon, a thing of barbels, scutes. I dreamt that prehistory skulks in our lungs. That it left me. Or I left myself—swam over fields and highways, crested in rivers luminous, waterways of tarmac, metal, of blinding fluorescent light.

LV. Savannah, Georgia, USA, 2019: "You: out!" I stopped walking towards the gas station toilets, turned slowly. The man pulled on his cap. I paused, exhaled, nodded once. I edged past him, past the plaques and decals—*MY GUN, MY CHOICE, MY AMERICA; CONFEDERATE REBEL*—past the beef jerky and Slush Puppies whirring lurid, blue-red-green, back through the grubby glass door and into the heat. Sun knifed off the car's paintwork. I got into the driver's seat. A white family pulled up in a sedan. The father stepped barefoot onto the forecourt. Bending to pull on a pair of New Balance sneakers, he saw me setting the GPS for the next nearest gas station. He straightened, tossed the shoes aside. The man stared as I adjusted my seat, put on my belt, as I turned the ignition. Exiting the petrol station, I watched a Mazda 323 swerve through the entrance and park at such an angle as to block two pumps. The car sat—dark green, engine growling—like some great, old gator come to sun itself across the tarmac. The doors swung open. A Black family—parents, three children—rolled out prayer mats and knelt, forehead to worn wool. I signalled right, pressed my fingertips to the crucifix hanging at my chest, to my lips. I checked the rearview mirror: the family in silent prayer, the rusted hubs and taped bumper of the Mazda, the sun-bleached pumps, and the man—six foot, his kicked-about sneakers still limp at his feet as he looked, kept watch on my leaving.

LVI. That same morning, as I prepared to leave the hotel in Savannah, two male employees unlocked my room and slammed open the door. I stepped back from packing my bag. The two men stared: noise, movement, all followed by silence, by absolute stasis. "Routine check in line with the city evacuation," the manager mumbled. I didn't say a word, only nodded, swallowed as the men left.

LVII. Hours later on the highway, cars and fields slicking the windscreen, I considered the two events—the gas

station, the hotel room. They are strange, these inci-
dents. I tend to push them down, aside, anywhere not
near me. I still don't know how to take that morning in the hotel—threat, perverse curiosity, mishap?
I cannot know if the employees burst into my room
because I am queer and transmasculine. Yet, the oddity of it: Why throw the door open? Why not simply knock? That day, driving to Atlanta, my thoughts
dissolving in the rain, I did not know that a similar
incident would occur months later in London. Again,
no knock; again, the door flung open; but this time,
I would throw myself—wet, wrapped in a towel—
against the opening door. This time, I would carry
the bruise for weeks.

LVIII.   "To immediately remove and permanently cure a headache, however long-lasting and intolerable, a live black
torpedo [electric catfish] is put on the place which is in
pain, until the pain ceases and the part grows numb."
                    —Scribonius Largus, *Compositiones medicae*

LIX.   Fish—sign of the faithful, of holy multiplication.
Fish—a medicine, a cure, salve and salvation.

LX.   During Japan's Edo period, the country closed its
borders, preventing all migration and trade. Only
the Dutch were exempt. Their schooners brought
Chinese wares to Sakai, Japan, shipments that, in
the early seventeenth century, included the goldfish.
The first goldfish unloaded at Sakai were supposedly
purchased by a samurai in service to the Koriyama
clan, who devoted himself to their care. Similarly,
when Lord Yanagisawa's fief transferred from Kai to
Yamatokōriyama, Nara, in 1724, Yanagisawa brought

goldfish with him. He encouraged the breeding and keeping of these fish amongst the samurai class—an act credited with inaugurating the tradition of the Japanese goldfish. The history of goldfish breeding in Japan took an important turn after the fall of the Edo military government. With the disbanding of a feudal regime, the samurai found themselves unemployed and powerless. The successive Meiji dynasty compensated the warriors with five to seven and a half years of stipend income in the form of interest-bearing bonds. This allowed the samurai to buy land at a reduced rate and begin their own businesses. Goldfish rearing figured prominently, the pastime often being a samurai's primary skill after combat training.

LXI.   In Katsushika Hokusai's (1760–1849) woodblock print *Goldfish Vendor*, a boy rushes to his mother, bulbous vial in hand. A goldfish vendor crouches beside her tank, a round-mouthed net and bowl at the ready.

By the early 19th century, goldfish had become affordable pets for ordinary citizens. Every summer, they were a popular commodity because, psychologically at least, viewing fish swimming in delicate glass bowls tempered the heat.

—Minneapolis Institute of Art
accompanying text to *Goldfish Vendor*

From weaponry to fish, warrior to aquarist. The early aquarium—a salve, an unguent, these liquid globes, shimmering gold to cool the heat.

LXII.   Atlanta, Georgia, USA, 2019: Largely funded by a $250 million gift from Home Depot cofounder Bernie Marcus, the Georgia Aquarium opened in 2005. For nine years, it held the title of "world's largest aquarium" until Chimelong Ocean Kingdom opened its doors in Zhuhai, China, in 2014. I made my way to the aquarium entrance, queued. Gun check. Weapon check. An employee plastered a fistful of flyers and promo coupons into my hands. I filed inside. *POSE UNDER THE WAVE FOR A PHOTO YOU CAN BUY AT THE EXIT!*

LXIII.   Electric, pulsing, bluer than blue: there is a magnetism to aquarium water, closer to swimming pools than oceans, to the glare of television sets. I followed the entrance signs, turned a corner. The Tannoy crackled, boomed: *Georgia Aquarium is a world leader in whale shark research and conservation and the only facility to house whale sharks in the Western Hemisphere!* All around me, themed exhibits branched off a central hub. Sharks leapt over entrances, spray-painted fiberglass, laminated MDF: *TROPICAL DIVER, OCEAN VOYAGER—BUILT BY THE HOME DEPOT, COLD WATER QUEST, SOUTHERN COMPANY RIVER SCOUT, DOLPHIN COAST.* Graphic tees snarled over display tables as shark toys and octopus key chains clamoured from hooks.

LXIV.   I wandered across the central hub, the smell of hamburgers seeping oily through the banding cyan light. The Tannoy system surged on again—a chorus of dolphin clicks set to music: *Our studies helped pioneer the whale shark biosphere reserve in Yucatán, Mexico, and led to the first mapping of the shark genome!* Alongside facilities in China, Taiwan, and Japan, the Georgia Aquarium is one of the world's few aquariums to exhibit whale sharks in captivity. Confining the planet's largest fish in a tank comes with a high mortality rate. The Georgia Aquarium encountered this difficulty when two of its initial whale sharks died shortly after being enclosed—a detail the facility omitted from its PA system highlights.

LXV.   Skirting a tiered table of giant pencils and starfish erasers, I entered the *SOUTHERN COMPANY RIVER SCOUT* exhibit. Contemporary river tanks intrigue me—how they might be the closest experience we have to seeing the aquarium in its nineteenth-century form. To imagine a single room, tanks murky, sediment eddying to the movements of barbels, bream, pike. *GANGWAY, ROPE BRIDGE, ENTER AT YOUR PERIL.* Mock signposts jutted from resin rock. I ducked beneath netting and plastic algae, blinked as the tank light shifted—blue to moss green. Children jostled in a game of tag, sprinted between the tanks, screamed as they thumped the interactive screens. A boy ran flat into my stomach, looked up somewhat stunned, barrelled on. I wandered alongside carp, garpike—teeth-packed truncheons of fish. At the sign *STURGEON*, I stopped, peered at crests and whiskers gliding between rocks. A sturgeon inched, snout hesitant, toward the glass. Another shifted at the rear of the tank. I turned back to the sign: *First found in the Upper Cretaceous, some 146 million years ago, sturgeon have undergone such little morphological change that they are considered living fossils.* Two children ran past, one trying to pelt the other with a seal Beanie. The sturgeon twitched, retreated.

LXVI.   What is this part of me that does not recognise my body, that somehow feels detached from my physicality in this life? Maybe it is what some centuries have called a "mind," what contemporary clinicians refer to as "dysphoria." I spent my academic life collapsing dichotomies of mind and body, body and world. And yet, whilst those beliefs still stand, I cannot escape a sense of separation, cannot negate a form of division—prehistoric, tectonic—that grinds through who I am. I have always felt as if my body moves itself—possesses its own will, character, its own thoughts. I experience my body as other, but also as *another*. Slightly animal, otherworldly almost, a pulse and breath not my own. For many years, I never believed in an afterlife. Yet, the longer I lived at disjoint from my own body, the more I turned to theology—its language and imagery—as a way to find rough peace within these limbs. If we do live many lives, if we really can occupy body after body—this helped me reconcile to life in a body I do not recognise. My relationship to my body feels custodial, guided by archaic movement. As if, I—soul or spirit—must look after it, as if, in turn, this body will carry, will show and teach and guide me: how to reconcile all the elements of myself, how to hold them, play of light over hands. I've come to realise it's a slightly strange way to live, to lead one's life as if there are two of you. And yet, I do. People often ask if I feel male or female, where I lie on a gender spectrum, whereas, in truth, I just feel like a soul in a strange craft.

LXVII.   Mind, dysphoria: I dislike these concepts, too clinical, too sterile. They smell of bleach. But a soul—something ancient that speaks—this I can nurture. Prehistory, a living fossil—perhaps we all carry a sturgeon that slips from us in sleep.

Speaking Reliquary

During medieval Christianity's cult of relics, there existed a class of object termed the body-part or "speaking" reliquary. Fashioned from precious metals in the form of a limb—commonly an outstretched hand and forearm—these reliquaries contained the remains of saints, martyrs, or apostles. In some instances, the reliquary visualised the bodily origin of the relic: a metatarsal encased within a foot. With time, the hand and forearm became the favoured physiological form of speaking reliquaries, regardless of whether they contained items from other bodily sites. The prevalence of arm reliquaries from the twelfth century onward is attributed to their use in liturgical ceremony. By way of the arm reliquary, religious clerics were able to animate the holy body, anointing, blessing, and healing followers by the saint, martyr, or apostle's own hand.

*

In 1935, off Australia's Coogee coastline, two fishermen attempted to reel a small shark onto their boat. A fourteen-foot tiger shark leapt from the waters and attacked the catch, hooking itself on their line. One of the fishermen gifted the tiger shark to his brother—an aquarium owner.

A week later at the Coogee Aquarium Baths, the tiger shark vomited a bird, a rat, and a human arm—severed, rope fraying at the wrist, two boxers tattooed in shaky slate blue. Upon forensic investigation, it was confirmed that the arm belonged to James Smith—a bankrupt builder, former bookmaker, and boxer involved in illegal gambling rings in Sydney. Smith had gone missing earlier that month, and, after examination of the arm, it was established that the limb had been severed not by any shark, but by a knife.

Carried by sea, shark, and aquarium to the cold metal of an autopsy table, this arm sparked a protracted murder enquiry. And, though justice was not served—the prime suspect, Patrick Brady, acquitted after key witnesses died in strange circumstances—this arm, this relic, thrown into water and eaten by a shark, still emerged, its truth came to light.

What Manner of Land

Each December in Sicily's Syracuse, sixty men in green berets carry a simulacrum of Santa Lucia through the streets. Over twelve feet tall and sculpted from two hundred pounds of silver, the martyr towers above the crowds. A dagger pierces her neck. A reliquary glitters in her chest. One arm cradles a palm leaf, whilst the other extends a dish—a dish from which flames leap as the saint's severed eyeballs survey the townsfolk.

Venerated across Italy and Scandinavia, Santa Lucia, or Saint Lucy, is one of Christianity's oldest martyrs, perishing in AD 304 during the Diocletian persecution. Lucia's father, born to Syracusan nobility, died in her early years, leaving Lucia to the care of her widowed and ailing mother. In adulthood, Lucia, a devout believer, took her mother, Eutychia, to Saint Agatha's tomb—a pilgrimage that not only cured Eutychia of a bleeding disease, but convinced her to distribute the family's wealth as Lucia had long wished. Learning that Lucia was bestowing the family's heritage and jewels upon the poor, her betrothed denounced her faith to Paschasius, governor of Syracuse. Paschasius ordered Lucia to burn a sacrifice before his image. When she refused, he sentenced her to defilement in a brothel. And so it came to pass: Paschasius's guards went to escort Lucia from the governor's chambers and floundered. Lucia stood— impossibly, divinely—fast. The guards yoked a team of oxen to Lucia, but still the martyr could not be dragged. They heaped wood at her feet, set torches to dry logs, but the flame refused to take. Instead, Lucia addressed the governor, prophesied, "You will be punished, Paschasius. The Diocletian rule shall fall. Maximian's end calls." At this, Paschasius had Lucia's eyes gouged from their sockets, and a sword thrust through her neck. Blinded, silenced, Lucia died.

Other legends maintain that Lucia tore out her own eyes, sending them as a deterrent to an unwanted admirer. In both cases, Lucia's eyes are said to have been miraculously restored upon burial.

The patron saint of Syracuse and Perugia, Italy, Lucia's patronage extends to martyrs, virgins, authors, cutlers, glaziers, saddlers, stained-glass workers, and even salesmen. But, above all, Santa Lucia is the patron saint of sight, the blind, and is invoked against ocular diseases. In iconographic representations, Lucia's eyes blink from salvers, swivel within the saint's own palms. In a painting by Francesco del Cossa, they bud from a tree branch.

Presiding over sight and blindness, light and darkness, Santa Lucia is traditionally celebrated in the frostbitten, dead hours of the winter solstice, hours when she rises—guardian of Earth's longest, darkest night.

*

A SACK SLUMPS BESIDE A GRAVE.

I dig. The spade rings into snow-choked soil, reverberates through oak, beech, lime. I take a pocketknife, slash the sack down the middle, and shake it—sulphurous, searing—into the pit. Clouds of yellow pigment sweep through the trees. Crows squabble skyward, disperse. I brush yellow from my jeans, my T-shirt. Kneeling, I take an ex-voto from my pocket—eyes hammered in silver—push it into the heaped powder, and cover them both with earth. Beneath my feet, the soil burns.

I wake, walk to the bathroom sink. I click on the light—hazy, flickering. Yellow cakes my lips.

*

Royal Leamington Spa, UK, 6:30 a.m., winter solstice, 2013: Locking the door to my mother's house, I walked the ten minutes to the local swimming pool. The night still lingered, metallic, biting. Mist curled off the river—silver quickly followed by darkness. I pulled my Reebok windbreaker further up my face, pushed up the bank, and turned onto the gravel footpath. Some way off, beyond the trees, beyond the steep bank that saw walkers slide, almost fall into the churn, the river twisted between fields, glittering blocks of flats. As I watched the mist spiral above the tree line, I heard the crunch of trainers over gravel. In front of me, a man approached— white, six feet tall, light grey tracksuit, scarf wound about his mouth and nose. My breath caught. *Get a grip, Lars. It's just a man out walking.* I cleared my throat. Gone. Over. He kept walking, so did I.

Streetlamps pooled, splashed off the kerb. Now and then, the light poured across a car windscreen, rushed off the bodywork. Early that midwinter morning, I was minutes from reaching the pool, minutes from my day—months, years of my life—carrying on un-interrupted, when the man I'd passed decided I was the person he wanted to abduct. This man, who jogged back, whom I heard be-fore I felt—soft footfall, shadow, strange movement—this man who, under the smouldering orange of a streetlamp, wrenched me back by the mouth.

*

"There is the house whose people sit in darkness; dust is their food and clay their meat. They are clothed like birds with wings for covering, they see no light, they sit in darkness."

—*The Epic of Gilgamesh*

*

In 2014, scientists at Surrey NanoSystems revolutionised black pigment when they created Vantablack—a black fabricated by growing cultures of carbon nanotubes on aluminium foil. The resulting surface absorbed 99.96 percent of visible light, flattening all forms it covered. Infamously, the sculptor Anish Kapoor bought exclusive rights to Vantablack, a controversy that led fellow artist Stuart Semple to launch a rival, Black 3.0. Affordable, workable like acrylic paint, the product is available to anyone providing they sign a contract agreeing to withhold the pigment from Anish Kapoor.

In 2019, MIT scientists Brian Wardle and Kehang Cui unveiled a new "blackest black," this time absorbing 99.995 percent of all light. The colour—an accidental coincidence of their research—was engineered from growing carbon nanotubes onto chlorine-etched aluminium. The material's light absorption, coupled with its unprecedented heat-resistant properties, attracted the attention of the aerospace sector. The imaging equipment and telescopes used in aerospace research require coatings black enough to reduce excess glare from cosmic bodies, yet strong enough to withstand a rocket launch—a pairing that had proved difficult until now. When questioned about his team's discovery and the global search to create an ever blacker black, Wardle, professor of aeronautics and astronautics at MIT, simply remarked: "The blackest black is a constantly moving target. Someone will find a blacker material, and eventually we'll understand all the underlying mechanisms, and will be able to properly engineer the ultimate black."

*

A MAN, SUSPENDED IN LIGHT.

Or water, was it water?
Both, perhaps—light shattering softly through dark lagoon.
The images keep slipping from me.
Only one surfaces—whole, glassy, blindingly bright:
An oleander hawk-moth emerges—hesitant, twitching—from the
man's mouth.

*

I remember the leather of his glove. Cold, blunt force. Blood. His
hands clenched my teeth, tongue, throat; yanked my windbreaker
until I choked. And our bodies, all the while our bodies bathed in
lamplight—amber, liquid in the carbon night. I remember that I
screamed. That, even then, I didn't recognise the sound as coming
from my own mouth. How it tore my lungs, my whole chest, more
chemical blister than breath. The man dragged me into a thicket.
Though I do not remember being dragged. I simply remember coming to, my body no longer on the path. The unevenness of earth,
grass. *I'm going to die.* The world empty—inky, vacuous. *Maybe,
he'll just rape me. If he just rapes me, that'll be okay.* The world
empty, save a deer—ochre bolt—disturbed before sunrise. And the
constellations—gateways in some eternal night.

*

"In the beginning when God created the heavens and the earth, the
earth was a formless void and darkness covered the face of the deep,
while a wind from God swept over the face of the waters."
                —The Book of Genesis 1:1–2, New Revised Standard Version

*

A race to buy unparalleled pigment, to somehow "own" a lack of light. A desire to launch Earth's "blackest black" into the single darkest environment known to humankind. And the utter confidence that we can engineer this so-called ultimate black, grow total darkness in a lab. As if this were an entirely new concept, this human invention of pure darkness, as if a total lack of light could ever be modelled by us and not by Hades' hands.

When I think of absolute darkness—that which begins us, ends us—it devours sound, smell, obliterates the world, oneself. A void that licks away your fingertips, your whole arm as you reach into it. Immeasurable weight. Infinite, impossible space. A night of rivers and jackals and whispering waters. A fear, a waiting death that pulses within our own chest: heart, kidneys, stomach—marbled in pitch.

Maybe in physics darkness equates to the absorption of all visible light, to a pure absence of colour, but not in the raw, hot breath of living. That winter morning, shadows creasing my clothes as a stranger dragged me over dirt, that morning turns in my memory: black, blue-black, green, umber, amber-black. That darkness is a gasoline spill. A hornet behind my eyes.

*

"When he opened the sixth seal, I looked, and there came a great earthquake; the sun became black as sackcloth, the full moon became like blood, and the stars of the sky fell to the earth as the fig tree drops its winter fruit when shaken by a gale. The sky vanished like a scroll rolling itself up, and every mountain and island was removed from its place."
    —The Book of Revelation 6:12–14, New Revised Standard Version

*

The deer stood a moment, snout, hindquarters quivering through the mist. The man hauled me towards it. *Rape, just rape.* I had never seen a deer near the public swimming pool, not in over a decade of walking along that route. The man grunted, kicked my ribs. My body winced. The deer bounded into the overgrowth. *Not murder, as long as it's not murder.* Grasses, heavy with dew, swept the blood haphazardly from my lips—extreme unction from a sky descended.

My limbs scudded over soil, numb things of night air, fading lamplight. My body relinquished, until a thought—somehow my own and not, with a strength I didn't recognise—detonated: *No.*

I heaved against the man's grip, pulling myself from the ground. The man staggered. I tore at my windbreaker zip. My jacket burst open, ripped off my torso, the man still grabbing at the pack, the jacket, my T-shirt—his fingers slipping, missing. I ran. Outside the pool entrance, my jeans bunched about my thighs, my T-shirt seams split, I wheezed, spat blood, dry wretched. My body searing under strip light, I pulled up my jeans and pushed open the foyer door. I walked past a queue of people waiting listlessly to enter. A woman talked about the new towels she'd bought for the bathroom. A man shook hands with other regulars. I tapped the reception glass.

"We don't open for another five minutes."

"I need you to call the police."

*

A MAN HANGS FROM A RAFTER BY HIS BANDAGED FEET.

Clay floor. Stone walls. A room that smells of forest. No abattoir.
Yet his body—navel to clavicle—sliced open.
And soil, not viscera, tumbles from his abdomen—leaf mulch, humus.
Who eviscerated this man? I remember no knife, no one else.
I only remember the mound of earth beneath his body—skin rent, fluttering like polythene sheeting.

*

I often think of the body as land—tectonic, silting—a thing of peat and loam. Of memories as mulching, slowly fossilising within limbs. My body remembers that morning, stores it—quiet, pulsing—deep in the sediment of itself. Abruptly unearths it—gnarled, bursting store of water and fats. Sometimes it takes an entire morning for the glove to reach inside my mouth. Sometimes all I hear are the birds bursting skyward. Sometimes the strip lights in the pool throb, the electricity splintering; other times, they taste of my own blood—ferrous, ringing.

To know a body—its limbs, muscle, sinew—as layer upon layer of living, as warmth, sheet rain, as occasional flood. Fertile. Cankerous. Knotted mass of root and tuber, of mineral salt—the grind and split of slow internal movement. And this memory—filmy, iridescent, unmarked save the occasional water vole, tar-clotted, at its edge. It disturbs me to think that I am stumbling around out there, shoes sliding in mud, skin smattered in blood. How this memory has taken root, grows steadily, imperceptibly. How it lives.

*

"What manner [of land] is this into which I have come? It hath not water, it hath not air; it is deep unfathomable, it is black as the blackest night, and men wander helplessly therein."

—*The Egyptian Book of the Dead: The Papyrus of Ani*
(Book of Coming Forth Today from Night)

*

At the station, the police officer swabbed my lips, inside my mouth. She rolled the Q-tip around my eye sockets, over the lids. Nose, cheeks, neck. She gestured across at the toilets: "You can wash up now." A couple of night shift employees talked of birthday parties they had to attend, cruises they couldn't afford. They made tea, yawned. I pushed through the toilet swing door, walked up to a basin, and lathered my face with a pink hand soap that smelt of marzipan. I fumbled for the paper towels, slowly blinked the police officer back into focus. "All good? Room's this way." Tube lights illuminated three polyester chairs and an imitation wood desk. Two police officers sat across from me. One handed me a mug of tea, its porcelain branded: *AXA, REDEFINING LIFE INSURANCE.* "So, tell us, clearly, from the beginning: What happened?"

I struggle to put that morning into language, into linear narrative. Certain gestures linger, only to then whiplash, distort what came next, my mind underwater. I remember the glow of a streetlamp, my body dragged into cloying, choking dark. I remember it as chest pain, sweat, as searing, ragged breath. I remember it as the kind of fear that makes you want to vomit. That, when it's over, actually sees you do so. As a body convulsing. As not caring if you shit or piss yourself. As not even knowing, at one point, if you have, because of the adrenaline, the shaking. I remember that morning as my ribcage unknitting.

After taking my statement, the officers drove me home. As the engine idled at an intersection, the male police officer turned in his seat, polyester scratching against polyester: "It could've happened to anybody. That area's a hotspot—rape, theft, GBH," the lights changed and he turned back to the road, glancing at me in the rearview mirror, "and no CCTV, it's a tricky one." The car eased off. I shifted in my seat: "Is that changing—CCTV, patrols, raised awareness?" The female police officer stared out the side window, tilted her head back slightly so I could hear better: "It's because you were on foot. You're twice as likely to be a target on foot. You should bike next time."

*

"There is a deeply cut cave, a hollow mountain, near the Cimmerian country, the house and sanctuary of drowsy Sleep. Phoebus can never reach it with his dawn, mid-day or sunset rays. Clouds mixed with

fog, and shadows of the half-light, are exhaled from the ground. . . .
No beasts, or cattle, or branches in the breeze, no clamour of human
tongues. There still silence dwells. . . . There are no doors in the palace, lest a turning hinge lets out a creak, and no guard at the threshold. But in the cave's centre there is a tall bed made of ebony, downy,
black-hued, spread with a dark-grey sheet, where the god himself lies,
his limbs relaxed in slumber. Around him, here and there, lie uncertain
dreams, taking different forms, as many as the ears of corn at harvest,
as the trees bear leaves, or grains of sand are thrown onshore."

—Ovid, "The House of Sleep," *Metamorphoses*

*

I LIE, BODY SUNKEN IN PEAT.

Rain. Pale light hazing through mist.
Lichen patterns my jaw, moss—the cotton of my T-shirt.
The air breaks: rush of wingbeats, caws.
I turn, breathing laboured. Ferns uncurl—up my throat, over
my lips.

*

I still see the deer in sleep, still catch myself in an orange hue, my
limbs moving within fur; still watch my own body—frenetic, loud, all
manner of smear and stain and smell—spill over the ground. I wake
to nausea: antlers grow from my abdomen; yellow smudges through
the pores of my skin. The bedsheets a snarl of blood, dirt, clotted
pigment. I sometimes wonder how much of myself I left there. What
parts of myself—skin, blood, sight—fell to soil? Slowly wound their
way through earth to the nearby riverbed? At the close of day, hours
exhaling from heat and noise, I think about who I was before that
morning, ask myself where that person is lying, turning, mulching

down. And it is in those same moments that I consider what of that place got tangled up in me—in my hair, my flesh—which elements dissolved into the bloodstream, ran right through me, calcifying down to the bone?

*

Several weeks after the assault, I tore the muscles from my right shoulder to my lower back while weightlifting. The inflammation bloated my torso to the point that none of my clothing fit. To wash, I stood beneath the dormitory's communal showers, passed the soap shakily over my skin. A friend helped dress me. Boxer shorts, an XL T-shirt, no shoes or socks as I couldn't pull them off again. The entire process took me an hour and a half. Doctor visits. X-rays. "Nothing to be done, just wait." Months later, my back hadn't healed, my body remained swollen. I couldn't swim, couldn't walk, run, ride a bike. I couldn't think. Eventually, after more medical vis-its, more referrals, X-rays, blood tests, one doctor said to me, "It's time to get used to this, to adapt."

I still wonder at that injury. How it happened performing a lift I'd completed for years. How the muscles tore on the same side by which the man wrenched me round. I cannot know if the assault led my body to collapse, if pain and fear sank into flesh and festered. Yet the injury always felt like an echo. That midwinter solstice—cankerous, rotting, briefly dormant before it resurfaced.

*

As I would explain to Gerald on the NHS mental health helpline, after he asked me why I didn't jump—a question that did not figure on the self-monitoring questionnaire—I remembered the man who had lifted me off the road, how I'd been convinced he was going to kill me, how I realised I didn't want to die.

"Gerald," I said, "I didn't want to get midfall and realise I'd made the wrong choice."

After a pause, Gerald replied, "Most people think of their loved ones."

*

When a trauma therapist asked me to explore the anger I bore this man, I drew a blank, my body rolling vacant.

That day, when I was attacked, the swell of the world carried me from anything I imagined for myself. I still consider the oddity of events, their tenuous links. If I'd cycled that midwinter morning, if bodies hadn't collided, come together bluntly in sweat, blood, vomit. In feral movement. Would I still have wound my way to that window ledge? And, if so, if I had still wavered several storeys above heavy traffic, where would I have fallen?

In the months following my aborted suicide, months when I struggled to speak, read, write; to think beyond degrees of hot-cold, pain-numbness; months when my back had me wincing in the bathtub, I woke sweating, lay on the floor panting, the room tilting, and I remembered that man, remembered that I wanted to live.

*

"Beyond the galaxies lies that primordial dark from which the stars shine out. . . . Today, as I write this, the Hubble telescope is photographing the very edge of the universe. The beginning of time. Worlds whose light has taken longer to get there than the existence of the Earth itself. Lurking black holes where time, space and dimension cease to exist. Will my voice echo till time ends? Will it journey forever into the void?"

—Derek Jarman, "Black Arts: O Mia Anima Nera,"
Chroma: A Book of Colour—*June '93*

*

My maternal grandmother and aunt, both Protestant, attend church every Sunday. My father, brought up a Baptist, never got around to the baptism. And my mother, escorted to Sunday school throughout her life, raised me an atheist as I attended a Catholic school.

Belief has always been a haphazard affair at home.

Years later, I still think of that man, not so much his actions that morning, but him—someone with a name, someone who eats, sleeps, catches rest under worn linen. Someone who loves. I'd like to ask if he ever thinks of that day. I'd like to tell him that I'm all right, good even. That I bear no anger. Which isn't to say I condone what happened. But that I hope he has help, that he no longer feels compelled to harm someone, harm himself.

I'd like to believe that coincidences might be concordances, echoes between bodies, actions at distance. That just maybe there is an order to things—distant, imperceptible—that something carries between us, something ritual, well-worn with a warmth of gold against skin. That the bodies we brush against can bring us things, be they easy or difficult, weighted or light. That faith might occur as movement, an effort towards slowness, softness, towards some kind of breadth. Obscure trust in the fall of one day into the next.

That day, my body dragged over cold ground, skin stained in mud, my own blood, I wonder if the earth was the one to impart sudden strength. Might this world—colossal, vital—bring one back to oneself? The vegetation remember, the ground bestow—ancient anointing of water, roots, of soil? To remember neither gold nor jewel as holy relic, but clay poultice—dirt followed by damp cloth. To consider the soil, its minerals, rotten leaf mulch as sacramental. As raw, elemental god. The divine not on earth, but of it.

*

"The waters are the *Gegenwelt* [counterworld] to the dry sphere of the waking day, into which the eye looks outward; in them the hidden nature of things is mirrored to the inner view. . . . Down into the water means down into knowledge. The ageless waters, taking all forms of nature, circulating as its life, know everything, they have been present since the beginning and conserve everything in their liveliness—nothing is forgotten."

—Heinrich Zimmer, *Maya: Der indische Mythos*

*

Now, when I look out at the night, it appears denser, darker than it did before. In places, my vision blurs between the real and the imagined. I might be walking home, glancing from a window across the backyards, but the night looms unnatural. In places, I swear, it swallows itself. I have grown used to it, slowly, across the years, this darkness that could hold a minotaur. And I know logically, in this era of microwaves and MRI scans, of probes, keyhole surgery, and satellites, that this is some echo of a traumatic event, some old weight that presses upon my eyes. But in that small time before sleep, as the night stains its way over this ancient sky, I let my thoughts drift, consider if there might be some arrogance to dismissing previous ways of seeing.

Where did they go, all the gods and the beasts? The jackals and winged horses, sphinxes and fish, all those creatures that weighed our organs in the afterlife, fed on years ill-lived? What do they tow now, those creatures that carried the sun and the stars, drew the moon to its place in the firmament each night? In those hours, I consider whether this world really is lined in shadow—thin veil between spheres. Whether, when our bodies plunge, drag against, and fray the weave, a kind of night bleeds—dense, resinous, vast beyond means. Maybe, it is in these moments when we almost cross over, when we believe we see the other side, that we blur the boundary between the living and the dead, that we bring a supernatural darkness back with us through the gauze.

*

Vantablack, "ultimate black"—experiments in a lack of light. But darkness has always existed, has done for as long as Earth has lived, roaming, unconfined by laboratory Petri dish. Preworld, under-world, death, grief, antimatter, black holes—our newest names for an age-old gateway—whatever we call it, however we get there, be it by boat, or tunnel, or flight; even if we must spiral outwards for mil-lennia, right out to where the universe strains at its own fabric: we find it—an ultimatum, unfathomable, inescapable, yet amorphous as supernatural ink.

*

Stemming from the Latin *lux*, or "light," Santa Lucia comes as bea-con in name as well as martyrdom. Lucia is often conceptualised as a bringer of light, her significance understood somewhat simplisti-cally as that of luminous salvation: a saint to banish the darkness—terrestrial and metaphysical alike.

In Scandinavia, annual celebrations of Saint Lucy involve young girls dressing in white gowns and walking a crown of candles through the church or home—a rather sanitised version of Lucia's martyr-dom. But in northern Italy, tradition dictates that, each December, on the eve of her feast day, Lucia leaves children gifts as they sleep. In anticipation, offerings of food crowd side tables, doorsteps: coffee for Lucia, bread for Castaldo, her escort, and a fistful of flour for her donkey. But the event comes with one condition: no child may see Santa Lucia, for, if they do, the saint will throw ashes in their eyes, blinding them for the night.

According to this belief, Santa Lucia appears as a figure who deprives sight, who might bestow darkness as much as alleviate it. No longer conceived in simple opposition to darkness and suffer-ing, Lucia possesses a more complex, even tangled relationship to both. Her faith confirmed in violence, her martyrdom baptised by blinding, Santa Lucia is a light born of darkness as much as a light to banish it. She understands long nights and their disturbing gifts, how they bestow ways of seeing, sights that cannot be unseen. How, from darkness, strange beasts come lumbering: fanged, shaggy, matted. How they pant from one's mouth, how they bite.

*

LAST NIGHT, WASPS MADE A NEST OF MY BODY.

Eyelids, lips, skin thrummed.
The year's largest supermoon filled my window, light cascading across papery coffin, fevered movement.

Judgement Run Down as Waters

In his *Histories*, Herodotus recounts a failed alliance between Amasis II, pharaoh of Egypt, and Polycrates, tyrant king of Samos. As legend has it, Amasis, concerned by Polycrates' unnaturally good fortune, counselled the king against injuring the gods—jealous creatures that they are. Thus, the pharaoh advised Polycrates to cast away the item he considered most precious so that, by his suffering, he might escape the otherwise certain ruin that awaited him. Seeing this advice to be good, Polycrates long considered that which he valued most. Eventually, the king ordered a fifty-oared boat far out to sea, took an emerald-set signet ring from his finger, and hurled it into the chop. Returning to shore, the king grieved his loss.

Several days later, a local fisherman landed an exceptionally large fish. After salting and wrapping the flesh in muslin, the fisherman slung the beast across his back, carried it through dust, banding heat. At the palace, he made an offering of the fish to Polycrates, who immediately ordered it to be prepared for table. It was then, in the bowels of the palace kitchen, the fish gutted by a scullion, that the signet ring was recovered—wet, gleaming—from within the fish's belly. Polycrates saw divine will in these events, and wrote of his fortune to Amasis. But Amasis, seeing not divine will, but the tightening grip of fate, broke off an alliance with the king, who, as it turned out, would be murdered by a false ally, his body crucified and left to decay in the heat.

In another version of this myth, so angered are the gods by Polycrates' offering, they return the ring as before, in the stomach of a great fish, only to then take his son in a single night of illness, the boy suffocating as his lungs drown in fluid.

Created second only to light and darkness, its body divided to arc the heavens, water retains its celestial origins: The blue violence of unknowable knowledge. Tides that mete out archaic, Old Testament justice.

With the Moths' Eyes[1]

In the summer of 2014, I tore the muscles from my right shoulder to my lower back whilst weightlifting. After two months, the muscle tissue still had not healed. Doctors could not provide an explanation. As it turned out, I would remain bedbound for the next six months, that is, until an estranged family friend came to visit and recognised my symptoms as those of undiagnosed dietary allergies. Untreated, my body failed to absorb nutrients or heal damaged muscle tissue. Instead, my body slowly wasted in a process similar to that of gradual poisoning.

As a side effect of the injury—one that I still cannot explain—I lost the ability to speak, read, or write. Exhaustion, depression, burnout—I am not sure. But at first, I stuttered, then later, I simply

---

1. The title of this work originally appears in Virginia Woolf's essay "On Being Ill."

remained silent. As for reading or writing, I managed a line, but any more and I felt nauseous.

During those six months, I slept, took painkillers, and visited different medical departments, where I was told that no further treatment could be offered, that I should start adapting to life as I could live it, which was to say: unable to dress or wash myself without assistance. I moved back home and slept in my childhood room. My mother put photographs of artwork on the walls: a woman holding up a dead bird, a dog next to a man slumped in a ditch. She also installed a small television set at the end of my bed so that I could watch films.

I kept strange hours during those months. Stared at the photographs, the television screen—images flickering into one another.

"Natural bodies are divided into *three kingdoms of nature*: viz. the mineral, vegetable, and animal kingdoms.

"*Minerals* grow; *Plants* grow and live; *Animals* grow, live and have feeling, Thus the limits between these kingdoms are constituted."
                                    —Carolus Linnaeus, *Systema naturae*, c. 1735

Moss. Leaf mulch. The cut-caw of birds breaking sky. Green is turning a burning colour, then black. There is more: the tongue, the teeth, the licking—fur over gums wet with the breath of a body that watches your own.

Baku.

Chinese, Japanese folklore.

Created last of all the animals, from the unused limbs of other beasts. Body of a bear, claws of a tiger, tail of an ox, eyes of a rhinoceros. Protects against pestilence and evil, eats things seen in sleep. If unsatiated, eats desires and aspirations, hollowing the sleeper's body.

The sleeper train hissed out of the station. You walked the aisle, signal lights streaking the windows. In the economy carriages, the communal cabins had no running water or partition from the corridor. Below a window, a fold-out table jutted between two bunks. Where one might expect a wall or sliding doors, the cabin gaped open, bunks of bodies yawning into the passageway. You found an empty cabin, took a top bunk. You lay back on the bedding, unfolded a blanket, slept.

A lamp glowed amber. Sat on the edge of a lower bunk, a man rested his elbows on the fold-out table. Arranged on the table: a bottle of vodka, the label—red, gold, and peeling; two mismatched glasses; an eight-ounce block of cured meat; and a knife. The knife and the meat rested on a square of cheesecloth embroidered at the corners. You shifted, rubbed your face. The man looked up at you, then back at the table.

Unscrewing the vodka, he began to speak—his voice slow, accented.

He said he'd been wondering when you'd wake up, that you'd been talking since the last station stop. He asked if you often saw things in sleep. And, then, as the man filled one chipped glass after the other, he told you about a remedy for troubled sleep, an old one, where you dig a hole and speak what you saw into the ground. Then, you cover the hole, pack it tightly with earth, and you wait for the ground to swallow those things, break them into something else. He said how they'd not come to you again after that, how you'd sleep easy—blank.

The man screwed the cap back on the bottle.

Said he knew it wasn't much use to you on a train, but still. He worked on the roads, and, when the diggers were chewing up the topsoil, he'd think about the dirt and the loam undoing themselves, things falling out. He spoke things into the road sometimes, the other men, too. Custom said a road wouldn't last otherwise, that the ground needed to be turned with things still alive if the quick-lime and asphalt were to hold for a long time.

The man cut slices from the meat, wiped the knife on the cloth.

Not that there was much construction work going at that time of year, he said, not with the ground all ice. And that's when the man said to come drink with him, said he was heading east for the winter fishing, said: "Tell me what you saw tonight, and I'll take those things with me. I'll speak them into the water for the pike to eat."

Asclepius.

Graeco-Roman mythology. God of medicine and healing. Also referred to as Oneiropompos or "sender of dreams."

c. 350–300 BC. Shrine of Asclepius, Epidaurus, Greece. *The Case of Sostrata of Pherai*. Bedridden, Sostrata of Pherai was carried to the sanctuary on a makeshift stretcher, where she slept, but did not dream. Awaking unhealed, she was carried homeward until Kornoi. There, a man stopped her attendants and instructed them to set the stretcher on the ground. Cutting open the sick woman's abdomen, the man pulled creatures from her body, dropped them— slick, writhing—into a foot basin. The basin was emptied, refilled. The man sewed Sostrata's abdomen closed, stood revealed as Asclepius—god of medicine, healing, rejuvenation, and physicians.

Iamblichus, *Theurgia*, c. AD 250–325, trans. Georgia Petridou: "In the temples of Asclepius diseases come to an end by means of divine dreams; and, because of the order of nocturnal epiphanies, the medical art consists of sacred dream visions."

In one bowl, the fruit is plastic; in another, it is glass. The plastic fruit has been put in the dining room; the glass—in the kitchen, where the window cleaner is kept. A telephone sits beside ceramic cockatoos. Every room in the bungalow is fitted with the same carpet: maroon, patterned with split-leaf palms in electric blue.

On the living room television, footage of the 1940 Tacoma Narrows Bridge plays out. The bridge is made of steel and concrete. It rolls like water in a basin. The voiceover explains the bridge's collapse: *All physical objects possess resonant frequencies or kinds of "pulse." When made to oscillate at these speeds by an external force, both object and external system fall into a feedback loop of increasing vibration. In physics, this is known as the phenomenon of resonance. In the case of the Tacoma Narrows Bridge, the "pulse" of the wind syncopated and then escalated with that of the bridge: the gale caused the bridge to vibrate at its resonant frequency—the wavelengths of object and environment amplifying one another, until physical boundaries were rent.*

Circadian rhythmicity.

Princeton University, New Jersey, USA, 1960s: Colin Pittendrigh leads study into hatching patterns of fruit fly larvae. Observes that larvae tend to hatch in groups at twenty-four-hour intervals. Repeats study with larvae raised in continuous darkness. No such rhythm recorded.

More larvae bred in darkness. A bulb flashes, once only, over the larvae: flies emerge—together, every twenty-four hours.

The greater wax moth has the most acute hearing of any known animal, perceiving frequencies of 20 kHz to 300 kHz. Comparatively, the human body is only able to detect sounds between 0.02 kHz and 20 kHz, our audible range cutting off where the greater wax moth's begins.

A radio speaks into a bedroom. The words drift across a desk. A fan heater carries the words upwards: they circle loosely, fall. A freight train passes; the words shudder. A late-night programme comes on the radio. You finish up, switch everything off.

A freight train passes; it shunts you back into the bedroom. The train gives way to the heating, an electrical bleep, your breathing. You sit up in bed. The radio clock display is hard-red [04:00]. You click the light on: the room camera-shutters awake. The air vibrates with moths.

"Earth's low frequency isoelectric field, the magnetic field of the earth, and the electrostatic field which emerges from our bodies are closely interwoven. Our internal rhythms interact with external rhythms, affecting our balance, REM patterns, health, and mental focus. [Schumann resonance] waves probably help regulate our bodies' internal clocks, affecting sleep/dream patterns, arousal patterns, and hormonal secretion."
—Miroslaw Kozlowski and Janina Marciak-Kozlowska
"Schumann Resonance and Brain Waves:
A Quantum Description," 2015

"In days of Spring the pulse is superficial, like wood floating on water or like a fish that glides through the waves. In Summer days the pulse within the skin is drifting and light, and everywhere there is an excess of creation. In Fall days the torpid insects underneath the skin are about to come out. In Winter the torpid insects are all around the bone, quiet and delicate like the nobleman."
—The Yellow Emperor's Classic of Internal Medicine
c. AD 1115–1234, trans. Ilza Veith

A man notes his heart rate and dates it. If it's within a certain range he writes in blue, if it's outside the range—in red. A species of bird is pencilled beside each entry whose wings beat at the same rate.

January 16.   60 BPM. *Cathartes aura.*
February 2.   138 BPM. *Erithacus rubecula.*
March 23.   124 BPM. *Corvus brachyrhynchos.*
April 3.   165 BPM. *Milvus milvus.*

Six months later, his obituary notes that he was a reputed ornithologist, and the coroner's report—that he died of a heart attack owing to a pileated woodpecker in the chest.

Liquid drains from a patient's lungs into a clear plastic container. Sediment collects at the bottom of the container.

Clipping an X-ray onto a light box, the radiologist circles an algal bloom in the lower right lung. He adds the X-ray to the dermatology report that notes patches of lichen on the abdomen, ribs, and back.

"We must purge and move such humors as are concocted, not such as are unconcocted, unless they are struggling to get out. . . . When one wishes to purge, he should put the body into a fluent state."

—Hippocrates, *Aphorisms*
c. 400 BC, trans. Francis Adams

A bathroom: rosy pink, glazed ceramic. Tube light: frosted, nylon pull cord. A cabinet: painkillers faded to unbranded, curved scissors, brown-bottled antiseptic, bandage, toothbrush, razor, soap— dirtier than expected. A mirror: rusting at the screws, streaked. A sink: filled with cold water and ice cubes, a body leant over it, face submerged; the body coughs, wheezes. The body straightens up, it looks at itself in the mirror, chokes slightly. The body pulls a three-spine stickleback, thrashing, from its throat. It drops the stickleback into a bucket of water. The body watches the fish in the bucket: silver, red plastic. The body stands, submerges its face in the sink again, and opens its eyes as underwater it spits rosy pink against the ceramic.

Shopfront. Blue neon: *TVS USED & NEW* hovers beside a bulb killing flies. Beneath this, black-and-white: an image stacks around itself on different-sized screens [*Sanyo, Panasonic, Sony*]. A German shepherd, twelve times over, drinks. The dog is stood in a wasteland; water covers the ground.

Further back, towards the counter, the same landscape plays on 42-inch HD. There is no dog. Instead, a man, knees to his chest, lies slack and wet. His body is also multiplied. It shivers—once, many times.

The German shepherd jumps down from the TVs, finds the man, and lies against him. Grayscale turns Technicolor: the screens now wet as neon-blue light.

Animals make their way to where you lie in bed. They grunt. They have horns and tongues, have hair. They shift shank. They are wet. You smell their sweat and your own. They are made to another scale: thrice your size at least. You watch them inhale. You are unsure what to do. You want to know how they got in—the door, the stairs, the landing. But you figure there's no point in thinking that. Instead, you get slowly out of bed. The animals do not move. You pull on a jumper, half expecting them to have gone once it's past your head. But they are still there as you put on some socks. And their breath fills the air, as, slowly, you let yourself stare at fetlocks and cannon bones, at flanks. You are no longer unsure of what to do. These beasts have come to you. You will house them.

Last Night, the Sea Spat My Body

LXVIII.　Salt-streaked, limp, upon a beach.
Sea birds pecked krill from my abdomen, sea lice
from my hair and skin.
Another image: Razor clams—soft mollusc torn from
olive shell.

LXIX.　For nearly two centuries, history has credited Dr.
Nathaniel Bagshaw Ward and Philip Gosse with the
invention of the aquarium: Ward with the tank itself
in the form of his "Wardian cases" (1836), and Gosse
with the concept of the public aquarium proper in his
founding of London's "Fish House" (1853). However,
writing in the *Giornale Letterario dell'Accademia
Gioenia di Catania* in 1834, Italian chemist Carmelo
Maravigna credits Jeanne Villepreux-Power with the

invention of the aquarium—a sentiment echoed in 1858 by eminent palaeontologist Richard Owen, in his *Encyclopaedia Britannica* entry on Mollusca:

LXX. "Madam Power invented three kinds [of aquaria]: one of glass, for preserving and studying living Mollusca in a room; another, also of glass, for small Mollusks, protected by an external cage of bars, in which they could be kept submerged in the sea, and withdrawn at will for inspection; and a third kind of cage for larger Mollusks, which could be sunk and anchored at a given depth in the sea, and raised, when required, for the purpose of observation and experiment."

—"Mollusca," Richard Owen, *Encyclopaedia Britannica*

LXXI. Jeanne Villepreux-Power cut an unlikely figure for a future pioneer of marine biology, excepting a certain determination of spirit. An eighteen-year-old cobbler's daughter living in Juillac, Corrèze, she had little involvement with the sciences. Instead, in 1812, she walked to Paris—a journey of over 250 miles—to pursue her career as a seamstress. In 1816, she achieved considerable recognition for her embroidery of Princess Caroline's wedding gown commissioned for the latter's marriage to Charles-Ferdinand de Bourbon. Shortly after this success, Jeanne Villepreux met and married James Power, a successful English merchant, with whom she relocated to Messina, Sicily, in 1818. Here, Villepreux-Power began her scientific observations and inventions of aquaria or, as she referred to them, "cages à la Power."

LXXII. By aid of her inventions, Jeanne Villepreux-Power hauled specimens in and out of the water, transferring them to a parlour tank, where she made several important advances in marine biology. Devoting herself to the study of cephalopods, in particular the paper nautilus or *Argonauta argo*, Villepreux-Power demonstrated that the creature did not find and inhabit a shell as French naturalist Ducrotay de Blainville maintained. Instead, the paper nautilus formed its own shell, repairing it in the event of damage. Villepreux-Power described how the *Bulla lignaria* preyed upon and digested the *Dentalium entale*, grinding the latter by way of a strong gizzard. She also noted tool use amongst octopuses—as one does by way of a busy schedule.

LXXIII.   In 1838, Villepreux-Power loaded her cabinet of scientific drawings, writings, and specimens aboard the brigantine *Bramley*—a cargo ship tasked with delivering her findings to the London Zoological Society. From the Messina quayside, Villepreux-Power watched six years' work set sail. She imagined it cresting through yawning blue and gathering storms. She saw the crates heaved onto London's docks, driven through smog and filth and pedlars' cries, saw them unpacked, beheld by London's most eminent men of science. But the ship never reached London. Last spotted off the Cape de Gatt, Spain, the vessel disappeared—no further sightings, not a crew member to tell of what happened. On February 5, 1838, the ship was presumed foundered with the loss of all hands.

LXXIV.   Villepreux-Power's observational records and scientific drawings were never recovered. Years of work plunged beneath the sea's surface, air pluming from the trunk. Proof that the paper nautilus grew its own shell. Proof that a dressmaker, who once walked 250 miles for her beginning in life, a woman who hypothesized and invented ahead of her time, kept tame beech marten as pets, proof that she might deserve credit for the nineteenth-century aquarium—all now deadweight, the paper bloated, leached of ink.

LXXV.   And yet, is this a fitting requiem for a cabinet of marine curiosities plundered without consent? After all, the sea tends to relinquish at a price. Years of lugging cephalopods into drawing rooms, of detailing the ocean's depths. Perhaps, the water had a pact with Villepreux-Power. A decade of scientific endeavour, a fateful few hours: the sea giveth and the sea taketh.

LXXVI.   Following the shipwreck, Villepreux-Power never conducted research again. In 1843, she and her husband left Sicily, splitting their time between London and Paris. Fleeing the Prussian army's 1870 siege of Paris, Villepreux-Power once more travelled the 250 miles to her hometown of Juillac, France, where she subsequently died in 1871.

LXXVII.   It would take until 1997, some 159 years after her signature drowned, for her name to reemerge: when the *Magellan* probe discovered a crater on Venus, scientists baptised the find Villepreux-Power. A name resurrected, trawled from salt and sand. A name cast—spiralling, colourless, soundless—into vapour, sulphurous clouds racing over carbon dioxide gas. A woman known for inventing aquaria, for her investigations of cephalopods. And a planet—the hottest in our solar system—whose surface air pressure is ninety times greater than Earth's. Thus, to stand on

Venus is, by equivalence, to dive three thousand feet into the ocean.

LXXVIII. There stands Villepreux-Power for as long as human memory and another generation's records endure— these computer systems we think of as immortal. Until some other form of shipwreck occurs, carries her into new, ephemeral orbit.

Ink

With the exception of Cirrina and Nautilidae deep-sea octopuses, cephalopods release ink, usually as an escape mechanism. Behaviours range from releasing large, disperse clouds of ink as a smokescreen to producing mucus-dense decoys, or pseudomorphs, to distract predators. Ink colouration varies between cephalopod species and depends largely on melanin levels. Octopuses produce black ink; squids, blue-black; and cuttlefish—varying shades of brown, or, as their Greek name suggests: sepia.

Unlike the naturally coloured ink of cephalopods, human tattoo inks have employed all manner of unlikely colourants, from soot, dirt, blood to animal and vegetable glues. An ancient recipe for tattoo ink by the Byzantine physician Aëtius of Amida even calls for one pound of Egyptian pine bark, two ounces of corroded bronze ground with vinegar, two ounces of oak-gall, or wasp egg deposits, and one ounce of vitriol. Thirteen centuries later, the ethnographer

Wilhelm Joest discovered just how unusual tattoo colourants could be, when, on April 7, 1871, he received a tattoo on both arms in Yokohama, Japan. Joest subsequently noted acute pain in the bones, a side effect of the red pigment—a vermilion acquired by adding the toxic heavy metal cadmium. Commercial tattoo inks today may contain a blend of iron oxides—which is to say rust—metal salts, and plastics. As in nineteenth-century Yokohama, particular colours require that heavy metals be added to the ink.

One colour of tattoo differs from all others: black ink fades beneath the skin. The issue lies in the way black pigments—particularly older black inks—are achieved by means of concentrated dark blues and greens. Over time and exposed to ultraviolet radiation, the pigment breaks down, slowly aging with the skin, black clouding, squid-like, to blue-green.

Anything That Makes a Mark,
Anything That Takes a Mark

After falling ill and losing the ability to speak, read, and write, I tattooed my body with text. In the slow hours of an attic tattoo parlour in Scunthorpe, Northern England, midwinter light bleeding through the windows, bar heaters humming in the corners, the men who worked on me gave over to talk. They explained how the skull is the most painful bodily site for a tattoo, even more than the eyeballs or genitals, there being almost nothing to separate needle from bone. They talked of how some parts of the body don't hold ink indefinitely. The soles of the feet shed too much skin, sloughing tattoos in a decade. And they explained how a body can reject the ink, that once, a client had demanded several tattooists work on him for a day. How his body went into shock, ran a fever, convulsed. Overnight, the ink bled out. The skin healed without a trace.

*

The English word *tattoo*, attributed to the writings of Captain Cook in 1769, originates from Polynesian languages, such as the Marquesan *tatu*, meaning "puncture" or "mark upon the skin," or the Tahitian and Samoan *tatau*, literally "to strike." Maori tā moko differs from many tattoo cultures in that the skin is not punctured, but carved. Pigments include awhato (a dye derived from mummified caterpillars killed by the *Cordyceps robertsii* fungus), scorched timbers, and the soot of burnt kauri gum mixed with fat. Stored in special jars, the pigments are buried when not in use. As for the original implements of Maori tā moko, these included chisels of albatross bone mounted onto wooden handles that were then struck with a mallet.

In Japanese, several terms may render the English *tattoo*, the two most common being *horimono* from the verb "to engrave, puncture, incise"; and *irezumi*, from *iru*—"to put in, stow, admit, insert"—and *sumi*—"ink." *Irezumi* was reserved for punitive tattooing, with *horimono* denoting decorative tattooing by choice and engraved sword blades. These terms have since lost this distinction, with further synonyms including *gei*—"tattooing," *bunshin*—"patterning the body"—and *shisei*—"piercing with blue-green." But even in Japan, where skin tends to be pierced as opposed to sliced, the material emergence of tattoo practices cannot be divorced from histories of carving, engraving, from this undercurrent of chisel, mallet, strike.

Decorative tattoo culture flourished during Japan's Edo period (AD 1603–AD 1867) following improvements to woodblock printing and the publication of *Suikoden*—a Chinese novel of richly illustrated, tattooed heroes. Until this point, tattoos carried a degree of stigma owing to traditions of punitive tattooing. But with a new demand for decorative tattoos, woodblock artists began replicating their illustrations on human flesh. Their tools included chisels, gouges, and Nara black ink, allegedly the finest in all Japan and made from Nara city's temple soot.

Japan's Meiji period saw tattooing outlawed in an effort to perpetuate Western beauty standards. Tattoos once again assumed criminal connotations. Even after occupation forces lifted the ban in 1948, many public baths and fitness centres still refused—and continue to refuse—entry to tattooed customers, associating them with the Japanese Yakuza mafia. For this reason, tattoo artists have traditionally operated in a discreet, if not entirely underground, manner in Japan. Whereas European or North American tattooists often ink designs requested by a client, traditional Japanese tattooists consult with a customer, but draw a design of their own choice. If a customer dislikes or disagrees with the illustrations proposed, the tattoo artist reserves the right to decline service. Centuries after woodblock artists took to inking human skin, Japanese tattoo practices have retained their origins in the visual arts. The client's wishes remain of secondary importance, with the tattooist operating not only as master craftsman—a purveyor of commissionable skills or techniques—but also as master illustrator or artist, a creator of images, symbols, and compositions, of aesthetics that resist a logic of supply and demand.

*

Midlands, UK, to Scunthorpe, UK, 2015: The radio clock glowed into the bedroom: [04:37]. I washed, dressed. Picking up my bag, I stepped into the undissolved dark of a weekday morning. Oil slick, all of it. Buildings, roads—liquefied under the weight of a winter-dead night. At the railway station, the night staff smoked, bags readied for the end of a shift. Above the platform, a digital clock snapped seconds onto wet tarmac, left an afterglow that bled across the track. A nurse still in uniform leant against the brickwork, tugged on her coat. I blew into my hands. The sound of metal under tension echoed down the platform. A man shouldered his duffel bag. The train—dense, diesel, ferrous—roared into the station.

In the train, I pulled a book from my bag and flicked to a series of photographs in which a man stamped a river. Sat in the shallows of the Lhasa River in Tibet, Beijing-born artist Song Dong lifted a wooden seal above his head, slammed it down again. Water leapt— sudden column obscuring the artist's face. Nearly a cubic foot in size, the seal's base bore a carving of the Chinese character for water (shuǐ 水). For an hour in the year 1996, Song Dong stamped the Lhasa River, printed water with its name.

*

In his article "Stigma: Tattooing and Branding in Graeco-Roman Antiquity," C. P. Jones argues that the ancient Greek word *stigma* should not, as is customary, be translated "branding," such as that by a hot iron, but as marking by ink, in short, as "tattooing." According to Jones, branding was overwhelmingly restricted to cattle in Graeco-Roman antiquity, whereas punitive tattooing upon humans was a much more common practice. The mistranslations of *stigma* arose in the Middle Ages, when practices of hot iron brandings upon humans were common and tattooing was largely unknown except to travellers of Asia.

Recounting Xerxes' failed crossing of the Hellespont strait, Herodotus explains how the king's wrath was such that he commanded the waters be "whipped with three hundred lashes" and "a pair of fetters be thrown into the sea." Herodotus continues: "I have even heard that he sent branders with them to brand the Hellespont." Though, if one accepts C. P. Jones's argument, Xerxes did not send "branders" to burn the sea, but tattooists to ink it.

The Hellespont, 334 BC; the Lhasa River, AD 1996: tattoos carrying across the world's waters, morphing to waves, slow swirl of circular currents.

*

The oldest tattoos on record—fixed upon bodies of skin rather than water—belong to the mummified corpses of Scythians held in the State Hermitage's Department of Archaeology of Eastern Europe and Siberia, in St. Petersburg, Russia. Excavated by Sergei Ivanovich Rudenko between 1947 and 1948, three of the four bodies—one man and two women—were found in the Pazyryk barrows of the Altai Mountains in Siberia. The bodies date from the fifth to the third centuries BC. The final mummy held at the Hermitage was discovered by L. R. Kyzlasov in 1969 amidst a Khakassian burial site from the first century AD.

Hermitage restorers found the tattoos by accident in 2003–2004. Peeling back the Khakassian mummy's clothing, they uncovered indistinct blue drawings. After consulting with forensic scientists from the Military Medical Academy, the Hermitage laboratory staff photographed the mummies with infrared rays. The technique detected and clarified the tattoos based on the soot present within their ink: Tigers attacked horses; leopards pursued mountain sheep. Birds soared beside their hybrids—hoofed animals with beaks, occasional wings. In the dimness of a laboratory, some two thousand years since their being inked, scenes of mauling, of magic, a bestiary of real and mythical creatures sprang once more into vivid, ferocious life.

*

Indelible ink was originally created not for paper, but for human skin. Invented in 1962 by the National Physical Laboratory in Delhi to combat voter fraud, indelible ink contains silver nitrate in addition to pigments of either violet, black, or orange. Silver nitrate reacts with the salts in human skin to create silver chloride, marking the voter's hand until the inked skin cells are shed. This can take anywhere from a couple of days to several weeks.

But even outside of tattooing or body modification, skin and ink share a long and intimate history, with skin frequently supplanting paper as writing support. Employed alongside papyrus in ancient Egypt, the oldest animal skin or "parchment" scroll dates to 2550–2450 BC. The use of parchment and vellum—parchment's more refined, calfskin counterpart—spread across the Middle East by the sixth century BC. From the sixth century AD to the fourteenth century AD, animal skins were the support of choice in Europe. To this day, vellum is used for the creation of handwritten Torah scrolls and the writing of parliamentary acts by the governments of Ireland and Great Britain.

As much as tattoo cultures are rooted in the arts—drawing, engraving, carving—writing cultures are rooted in skin, in ink scored across flayed, soaked, dehaired, and stretched hide. To write was, and still is, in some sense, to tattoo, to ink script upon skin.

*

After three trains, a dozen stops, and several hours of slithering through a lightless morning, the train screeched into Scunthorpe station. On Station Road, a string of tinsel bunting zigzagged over a vacant lot, its line slack, its metallic fronds weathered and gapped. A Union Jack fluttered beside red and yellow acrylic: *SCUNNY CAR WASH*. On the high street, a man waited for the bet shop to open. A sales assistant dragged a swing sign onto the pavement. I kept walking, watched as, beneath the words *KING KEBAB*, a neon carving knife cut slices from imaginary meat.

A buzzer drilled me into the shop. The door closed with a jolt, sent a breeze coiling across floorboards right up to where an Anglepoise glowed atop a wooden counter, dust spiralling through its beam. A man called over his shoulder: "Just a moment." I scanned the room. Framed tattoo designs crowded the black walls: snakes slinked from skull eye sockets; *MUM* fluttered over bleeding hearts, sagged between swallows' beaks. A fluorescent green cobra hissed across the man's bicep. Purple dice tumbled down his forearm. The man straightened: "Right, how can I help?" I took the appointment card from my pocket, slid it across the counter. The man nodded: "Yes, you're the one who only wants text," the man tapped the card against the wood and walked over to a doorway, "unusual that, we get a few names or quotes, but all text—we've not had that before." Pulling aside a bead curtain, the man gestured:

"Straight up the stairs, first chair on your right. Jay's got the transfers ready for you."

Four leather tattoo chairs occupied the attic room. Drafting
tables lined the walls, submerged beneath inks, needles, vinyl gloves.
At the far end, floor to ceiling windows looked onto the street below:
women pulled tartan shopping caddies, smoked on benches. I
stepped up to the first chair, my breath faintly clouding. Jay clicked
on an electric heater: "Lars, right? Sorry about the cold, no central
heating."

Taking a sponge in one hand and a Bic razor in the other, Jay
daubed soapy water across my shoulder blade, drew the razor over
skin. He wiped, resoaped the shoulder: "Right, stand for this." I
swung my legs off the reclined chair. Jay picked up a sheet of what
looked like carbon paper: "Try to ignore the water and relax your
shoulders. The skin needs to sit naturally, otherwise the print will
go askew." Jay placed the hectograph over the wet skin, smoothing
the paper until it moulded to the shoulder blade. Peeling back the
transfer, he nodded to a couple of full-length mirrors: "Check the
placement's good. Don't worry if not, we'll rub it clean with alcohol and reprint." Standing between the mirrors angled so I could
see my back, I stared at my reflection in the glass, stared as purple
text hovered amidst patina, dust, paint splats. Akin to carbon paper,
hectograph paper allows tattooists to transfer a design onto a client's
skin—a nonpermanent outline over which a tattooist can ink. I
lifted my arm. The lettering twisted, my skin more mobile than I'd
ever realised, elastic, migratory, animal even. I returned to the chair.
Jay swivelled on his stool to face me: "All good? Great. If you lie
down with your arms by your sides, that way you won't stretch the
skin out of place. We don't want the ink travelling, enlarging onto
the ribs."

The leather chair pressed cold against my jaw. My head to one
side, I looked at the designs in progress crammed across the walls:
Shishas—beasts part dog, part lion—emerged from lotus flowers.
Koi circled cherry blossoms. In one corner, scarab beetles scuttled—

majestic, iridescent—from Anubis to Jörmungandr, from one world's jackal to another's serpent. The tattoo machine hummed above me. A fan heater lifted a few of the drawings' edges, tigers and dragons roaring in waves. The humming changed frequencies. I exhaled as the needle dragged its first line into my skin.

*

In a retrospective monograph of his work, Zhang Huan discussed his move from the flat surface of oil painting to the embodied form of performance art:

"I had discovered that my body could become my language, it was the closest thing to who I was and it allowed me to become known to others. I had been struggling with how to move from the two-dimensional, and then I discovered this new vehicle, my body."

12 Square Meters, 1994: In Dashancun Village, an east Beijing suburb used as the city's dumping ground, Zhang Huan covered his naked body in a paste of fish oil and honey. For the next hour, Zhang Huan sat—glossy, rancid, immobile—in the mouth of an open pit public latrine. Flies swarmed his body, crawled into his ear canals, into his nostrils, thrummed between the fine hairs of his skin. Maggots inched across the floor. Mosquitoes rose and fell, sluggish in the cloying midsummer heat. Insects flicked from Zhang Huan's body to urine, faeces, to soiled paper, and cigarette butts. Zhang Huan then walked from the latrine into a nearby pond, insects rippling off his body in rings.

65 Kilograms, 1994: White sleeping mats covered Zhang Huan's studio floor. Viewers sat, watched Zhang Huan's naked body sway ten feet above them, a smell of disinfectant settling over window ledges, piling into the creases of their own clothing. Gagged, bound, and hoisted into the ceiling by chains, Zhang Huan looked back— suspended face down, above a hotplate. A doctor climbed a ladder, inserted an intravenous line. Blood flowed into a plastic bag, dripped several feet, splashing into a metal pan atop the hotplate. For an hour, blood hissed on scorching metal, the room clouding with the vapour of Zhang Huan's frying blood.

Pilgrimage—Wind and Water in New York, 1998: P.S. 1 Contemporary Art Center courtyard. A Ming-dynasty daybed laden with slabs of ice. Tethered to the daybed, purebred dogs barked across a soundtrack of Tibetan prayer chants. Prostrating himself naked upon the gravel, Zhang Huan crawled to the bed and lay atop the ice, dogs and winter winds howling about his limbs.

In 2001, Zhang Huan dramatized the tension between two-dimensional and three-dimensional art forms in the performance piece *Family Tree*, a work that explored the power dynamics between individual and cultural identity, between body and language. Having recently moved to the United States, Zhang Huan commissioned three calligraphers to cover his face in culturally specific references. For several hours, calligraphers wrote Chinese proverbs, quotations from Chinese literary texts, the names of Zhang Huan's relatives, familial anecdotes, and words from the ancient Chinese art of physiognomy onto the artist's face. Documented in nine photographs at timed intervals, the writing increasingly mottles Zhang Huan's skin, blotches, obscures, until, eventually, it covers every facial feature. In the final image, Zhang Huan's face shines with fresh black ink.

Interpretations of this work tend to foreground the culturally constructed nature of individual identity. In its presentation of the piece, the Metropolitan Museum of Art writes: "Rather than elucidating Zhang's character and fate, these traditional divinatory marks ultimately obscure his identity beneath a dense layer of culturally conditioned references." Similarly, Phillips auction house remarks: "Ironically, the two practices in this work that are most deeply embedded in Chinese culture, calligraphy and physiognomy—or 'face reading'—nullify each other. When they are applied as a visual lexicon to Zhang's face, he is stripped of all his identifiable markers.

The nine photographs of *Family Tree* transform viewers into participants, allowing them not only to engage with Zhang's performance, but to reflect upon their own intrinsic and constructed identities."

Family Tree is read as an obliteration of the individual by cultural and sociohistoric context. It is understood as an enactment of language obscuring, even dominating, the corporeal. Language overwrites the body, negates its power as corporeal access point and expressive medium with the world. Critics rarely address the discomfort of the latter images: how, saturated in ink, Zhang Huan's face jolts the entire performance into the iconography of blackface.

Language might obliterate Zhang Huan's physical form, but the body cannot be controlled so easily. Despite the artist's conceptual intentions, his body carries the work into unwanted territory. Unruly, unforeseen by Zhang Huan, and unaccounted for by critics, the inked-out body migrates the piece from conceptual meditation on selfhood into racist lineage. Far from obliterated, unable to signify, or subservient to language, the artist's body speaks louder than any calligraphy. It screams.

*

One chair over, a heavyset man winced, a heart's shaky outline disappearing under fresh black ink. The tattooist paused: "Let's say we cover this tat, then you can have a cigarette, stretch your legs before I cover the rest of the forearm." The man nodded.

Jay glanced at my face, noticed me staring: "He's having blackout," Jay nodded towards the man, "black ink, nothing else. Swathes of it. Hurts like hell. It's scar over scar, see, tattoos essentially being healed wounds packed with ink." Jay frowned as he tattooed a serif: "And then it's the sheer volume. I mean, to puncture a whole forearm, inject an entire surface with ink—it's rough going. A lot of guys have to do it in stages. They start sweating; one guy clean passed out last week." Jay dabbed at blood, excess ink: "Not women, mind. Never had a complaint. It's the oestrogen, I think, got higher pain thresholds, better endurance. Some blokes, they think it's shit, but I tell them: for real, ten years in the business, not a yelp, no fainting, nothing. Higher percentage of body fat also helps—stops the needle hitting too near bone. But it's definitely not only that, I've had plenty of heavy fellas in here, and they still groan." Jay cleaned off the needle, flicked his wrist, pressed the needle back into skin: "Some say blackout's worse than the skull or ribs. Don't know, myself, I've not had it done. I don't want to erase what's gone." Jay shifted on the stool: "Like, that meant something to you once, even if the work's shoddy or the meaning's soured. I've always had old tattoos reworked. I see tattoos as mobile. I mean, generally, they already are, what with how the skin ages, slackens, how the line work warps or bleeds, how the colours degrade. But I think of designs that way too, not just the ink. I like to think of tattoos shifting across the skin, leaping into new pigments, evolving shapes. To see them accumulate, mutate."

*

My tattoos are taken from works I once knew intimately, but that I now can't read, words I recall more as gesture, as movement than as lucid argument. Writing as relic, rite, as ritual. A thing not to be read, but touched, sworn upon, housed in a body. I like carrying ink within my skin, how it smudges, dilates slate-blue. I like embedding the world tangibly within my limbs. The words of strangers—a low hum to my movements. An act to which the body bears witness.

Getting tattooed after my mind shattered, I wasn't simply grasping at, or trying to recover, some literate former self. I was, on some level, trying to score my body into the world. In rendering a formerly literate self as physicality, as ink to be stowed in fat and tissue, I insisted upon my body as new centre, as primary point of contact with world. Tattooing my body after I lost the ability to speak, read, and write was not a nostalgic gesture, but rather a movement away from language-centred meaning. A commitment to the slipperiness, the fleshiness of coming to the world, first and foremost, as a body.

*

"We spent all *Tuesday*, the Nine and twentieth of *April*, in getting Marks put upon our Arms, as commonly all Pilgrims do; the Christians of *Bethlehem* (who are of the Latin Church) do that. They have several Wooden Moulds, of which you may chuse that which pleases you best, then they fill it with Coal-dust, and apply it to your Arm, so that they leave upon the same, the Mark of what is cut in the Mould; after that, with the left hand they take hold of your Arm and stretch the skin of it, and in the right hand they have a little Cane with two Needles fastened in it, which from time to time they dip into Ink, mingled with Oxes Gall, and prick your Arm all along the lines that are marked by the Wooden Mould: This without doubt is painful, and commonly causes a slight Fever, which is soon over; the Arm in the mean time for two or three days, continues swelled three times as big as it ordinarily is. After they have pricked all along the said lines, they wash the Arm, and observe if there be any thing wanting, then they begin again, and sometimes do it three times over. When they have done, they wrap up your Arm very streight, and there grows a Crust upon it, which falling off three or four days after, the Marks remain Blew, and never wear out, because the Blood mingling with that Tincture of Ink and Oxes Gall, retains the mark under the Skin."
—Jean de Thévenot, "Of the Way of Making What Marks Men
Please upon Their Arms," *The Travels of Monsieur de
Thévenot into the Levant in Three Parts*

*

First recorded in the writings of Pliny the Elder, iron gall ink—a mixture of gall nuts, iron sulphate, water, and gum Arabic—became one of Europe's most ubiquitous writing fluids from the Middle Ages to the nineteenth century. But the inherently acidic, rust-coloured ink slowly corroded the parchment, vellum, or paper upon which it was placed, eventually destroying its own script. Supposedly immutable, even immortalising, writing faltered, degraded.

Tablets, parchment, paper, script: there is a certain permanence attributed to writing. And not without reason. Civilisations have, with the advent of alphabets, ensured the transmission of knowledge in large volume. In the case of Xerxes' tattooing of the Hellespont, or Song Dong's stamping of the Lhasa River, it is water's transience, not that of writing or ink, that makes itself most apparent. The administering of a tattoo or stamp upon water—of fixed entity upon mobile element—creates a startling juxtaposition between permanence and mutability, between written word and water. But Xerxes' and Song Dong's actions have a second, more surreptitious meaning at play: a juxtaposition of *supposed* permanence—Xerxes' whips, fetters, tattooing needles, and Song Dong's cumbersome wooden seal—against assumed mutability—river water. For, despite commonplace interpretations of water as transient, water endures. It outlives marks, brandings, surpasses inked language effortlessly. Whereas tattooing, stamping, written ink—there is always such instability there, in their materials, in their dependence upon bodies to bring them into being.

Growing up, I thought of language as permanent. I did not think that one day I would be severed from it, forced to renavigate how I approached it. As a master's student at the École normale supérieure in Paris, I would regularly read and write for thirteen, fifteen hours each day. But, later, when I tried to write again, words flooded—disparate, jarring—I couldn't filter or funnel them. I started small: shopping lists, postcards, notes left at home. I never wrote more than a couple of lines and I'd have the beginnings of a splitting headache. On rereading, I noticed they were littered with mistakes—spelling, grammar, punctuation. If language had once felt like water that rose and fell, parted when I needed, it now snarled, pulled in all directions. It was going to kill me if I kept climbing in.

Each time I wrote, it was the same—shattered parts of sentences loomed up through depth. Colours. Movements. An image. The hum of a filament. A fly hitting an element. Bluebottle killed by blue light.

I found my way back to writing by way of the visual arts. Not as linear one-word-after-another sentence, but as three-dimensional construction, as composition, lighting, texture, as sculpture and image.

I began treating the page as volume. Rather than working left to right, top to bottom, I wrote words into the space of the page, sequencing them intuitively. A colour might go somewhere near the top margin if it came dazzling. If fading—I'd pencil it into a bottom corner. Once, red came as a siren—*red, red, red, red, red*—blaring across the paper. *Run* might zigzag, and I, stumbling between each image or gesture that broke onto the paper, filled in the articles and particles, the linguistic dust and grout to make a sentence. Each sentence came like this. Fragmented, exploded. Built from the inside out.

Objects, situations—the choice of one dictates the next. I compose sentences through a textural, physical logic, a sort of curation in space. As if I were handling wax, felt, cotton, razors. Language, writing in particular, feels more visceral than it ever did.

In Song Dong's work as in Xerxes' punishment of the Hellespont, it is the stamping, the tattooing that reveal themselves impermanent, not the water—great immutable body that it is. Instead, script comes, falters, dies, changes. To consider language, then, a thing of tides. Entity that swells, crashes, drowns. That can ebb, suffer sudden drought.

*

A seminal ancient Egyptian medical text, *The Papyrus Ebers* (1550 BC, trans. Cyril P. Bryan) devotes considerable time to the question of bodily suppleness, listing salves for "hardenings." Likewise, the papyrus lists ointments for specific limbs: ass dung, honey, sea salt. But it is in a salve "to make everything possible supple" that a recipe calls for goat's fat, honey, vermilion, and "writing-fluid." As it happens, whether aqueous, liquid, paste, or powder, an ink requires two components: a colourant and a vehicle or "binder." A rule not dissimilar to the preparation of topical medicines.

That day in Scunthorpe, I remembered *The Papyrus Ebers*, this fleeting allusion to ink as medicine, rare salve. And watching Jay wrap my forearm in clingfilm, I wondered if millennia-old knowledge might bear out, if this ink injected into skin might rinse, cure, might prove miraculous unguent.

I shifted on the chair, clingfilm squeaking against leather. "Careful with the wraps," Jay gestured at the plastic dressings, "they're slippery at this point. But you don't want them tearing. You gotta keep those cuts clean." The room dimmed, the night pulling in, foaming, rushing. Jay looked out the window, chewed his lip: "How you doing?" I gave a thumbs-up. "Well, I'm going to get Charlie to help me on this last bit, otherwise you'll have been under the needle way too long. He'll do one tattoo; I'll do another. But you've got to be sure you're okay. It's cold, it's been nearly six, seven hours. The risk is, we do this and the body goes into shock. If that happens, the body will reject the ink, all of it, it'll all bleed out." I thought back to the months bedbound, my mind drowning, grasping at images, objects, colours. I stammered, "No trouble."

Soap, razor, hectograph. I lay back and stared at the ceiling. The tattoo machines began tracing—stinging, thrumming, great metal wasps at my collarbone and wrist. Jay looked up at Charlie: "You had that, someone's body reject the ink?"

Charlie squinted at my collarbone. "I did have one woman, a swimmer, she got a sleeve done. Swam in the pool every day for a fortnight straight after. Whole thing carried into water—hours of work, serious money—the chlorine leached the ink. She had to have it redone. I said to her, no water for a month this time. I guess I've not seen a body reject the ink so much as water steal it. But still, to see an arm you sent away stacked in ink, to see it clean again, the skin healed—it unnerved me, as if I worked in ghosts."

*

Bedbound for months, I watched pale images blink across a bulbous television set. I stared at photographs plastered on my bedroom walls. Even as my physical state improved, I did not write, did not read. For a year, I only looked at fine art books, at pages that spoke back in ways I understood: a woman holding a dead dove; brass organs atop brass boxes; a resin cylinder—matte blue, perfectly reflective top.

In his oft-quoted book *On Writing: A Memoir of the Craft*, Stephen King comments: "If you don't have time to read, you don't have the time (or the tools) to write. Simple as that." There are many such maxims on reading and writing. How no one can be a good writer without being an avid reader. How to not read is always to be ignorant, linguistically unskilled, lacking, is to have nothing to say. And yet, I find myself unable to read in the strict ways I once did. Reading is now a practice to which I am barely tethered; that, occasionally, lets me in, shuts me out soon after.

For months after falling ill, I tried to read—a book, a chapter, a page. Inevitably, a few lines in, I'd feel sick. A year later, I managed one book across several weeks—each chapter only a couple of pages. Years later, I still struggle to read. I was more capable as a teenager than I am as an adult. I get headaches, lines swerve, shatter. I read the same paragraph two, three, sometimes five times. Often, I give up.

I'd like to think "reading" could be seeing, hearing, smelling, could be sensing the slip of a body through this world. That language might allow for strange syntax, ruptured sentence. That it might capture the friction between a body and its grasp on being understood. Though I find the loss of sustained reading and writing tiring, I have come to realise that I can work with these senses of lack. In many ways, they've shifted, not so much lost as mutated, warped under heat and duress. I'd like to think that those bodies, bodies that fail to adhere to norms of language, that don't manipulate words in the ways they are told they must, I'd like to think there is space for them, for me, to speak. That maybe experiencing the world as less worded, as gesture, vivid image, can be seen not as lack but as resource. That they can bring some unusual angle, strange value to writing, reading, to how we communicate.

*

After Jay and Charlie rubbed my skin with alcohol, dried it with paper towel. After they wrapped my limbs in clingfilm. After they eased my T-shirt over my lettered body, explained how to keep the ink covered, bathe without water splashing the scarring, how to rub and wrap the tattoos with fresh dressings. After I left these two men, one of whom had worked across my body, stretched and inked and pressed my skin for eight hours, I stepped into the dark street, walked past the kebab shop, its window now sizzling spit meat. And I thought back over the books I could no longer read, how they hummed now beneath my clothing, whispered against its seams.

For the last few hours of that day, the train blazing through fields, an occasional station lamp flickering into the night, I shivered against the polyester of an economy seat, travelled frozen, yet sweating, until I made it through my mother's front door, up the narrow staircase I'd walked since childhood. Until I collapsed into my old bed, clean cotton brushing against blotched plastic. Until I slept heavy, dreamless.

*

4:45 a.m., June 15, 2015, Huiyu Island Harbour, Quanzhou, China: A helium balloon—white, colossal, billowing—rose above the shoreline. It pulled 1,640 feet of explosives into the air. The artist Cai Guo-Qiang lit the fuse still trailing upon the ground. A ladder of quick-burning fuses and gold fireworks ignited, seared the indigo of the dawn light.

A project conceived to "connect the earth to the universe," *Sky Ladder* had been dogged for two decades by technical and bureaucratic issues. That early morning in Huiyu Island Harbour, Cai

Guo-Qiang finally completed the work in secret with only two hundred people in attendance—his fourth attempt in twenty years. As with the majority of Cai Guo-Qiang's works, *Sky Ladder* used gunpowder—a substance first created by Chinese alchemists in AD 850 as they endeavoured to produce elixirs of immortality. A fitting medium for a structure designed to connect us to the heavens.

For years, I attributed a definition of drawing to Cai Guo-Qiang: "anything that makes a mark, anything that takes a mark." The phrase appeared, scrawled across the inside of a notebook I had kept during months of convalescence—an odd mix of photographs, occasional words, exploded sentences. A notebook I recently re-read. For some reason, I remembered copying the quotation from the documentary *Sky Ladder: The Art of Cai Guo-Qiang*. I later realised this to be impossible as I abandoned the notebook long before the documentary aired. Nonetheless, I rewatched the documentary, two, three times. Still, no missed frames, no rediscovered trace. Cai Guo-Qiang never said any such thing. Implicitly, by the nature of his work—yes—but, explicitly—not once. Weeks later, I told my mother, a mixed-media artist and teacher, of the unattributed quotation I'd found in the notebook. She replied: "I taught students that concept for years. It's an old saying, that one. I taught you to draw like that. Either it was my notebook or you remembered it at some point, wrote it down—so second-nature as to forget."

*

Lines, dots, tone, colour, pigment. Carving, chiselling, engraving, puncture. And then—this manipulation of skin as canvas: piercing, grooving, packing with pigment. This inscription into the long and vital duration of the human body, production of live, living work.

A practice of marks, perspective, of relief work; of lived acquisition and exhibition, tattooing combines the imagistic, the sculptural, and the performative.

*

Eins und Eins (One and One), 2016: Dressed entirely in black, save a pair of immaculate white shoes, Melati Suryodarmo entered a white room in Singapore's Pearl Lam Galleries. A stainless-steel basin filled with black liquid rested on the white floor. Melati Suryodarmo sipped from the basin. The artist writhed, grimaced—teeth jet black. Gulping from the basin, the artist convulsed, spat the liquid—brown-black, smattering—over the white floor. For the next two hours, Melati Suryodarmo drank, spat, and vomited an ink-like substance across the gallery walls, floor, and ceiling. She writhed, flailed, groaned.

Performed as part of the group exhibition *In Silence*, *Eins und Eins* explored repressed speech, reimagining unvocalized language as festering, as bodily canker that must be expelled—fetid, violent. In *Eins und Eins*, Suryodarmo presents us with ink to be excreted. Words spat, regurgitated. Yet, here I stand watching recordings of *Eins und Eins*, here I stand agreeing, appreciating this expulsion, me, with my body of tattoos of books I can no longer read—ink to be stowed. Words forgotten, kept warm in tissues and fat.

*

"When we talk about books . . . we are talking about our approximate recollections of books. . . . What we preserve of the books we read—whether we take notes or not, and even if we sincerely believe we remember them faithfully—is in truth no more than a few fragments afloat, like so many islands, on an ocean of oblivion. . . . We do not retain in memory complete books identical to the books remembered by everyone else, but rather fragments surviving from partial readings, frequently fused together and further recast by our private fantasies. . . . Our relation to books is a shadowy space haunted by the ghosts of memory, and the real value of books lies in their ability to conjure these specters."

—Pierre Bayard, *How to Talk about Books You Haven't Read*

*

In his unfinished work *The Visible and the Invisible*—a volume cut short by a stroke aged fifty-three—Maurice Merleau-Ponty remarks upon the need for a new language of the body, one that doesn't follow divisions of mind-body or body-world. Something elemental, spatial. A language of pivots, of movement.

Years ago, in that tattoo parlour in Scunthorpe, Jay pressing one of the hectograph prints to my spine, he asked, "So what language is this one, French?" I nodded. The quotation came from Merleau-Ponty's unfinished last work—a book that, for years, I lugged onto trains and buses and boats, a book that had littered my desk, crowded my luggage, a book that underscored the corporeally informed nature of thought, a book that, once my mind slipped and I'd no longer been able to read it, had ruffled atop my bedcovers—a talisman, a touchstone. Jay peeled back the hectograph: "So, what does it say?" Sitting up, I looked at the fluttering hectograph. I blinked. Following the words with my forefinger, my throat full of moths, I stuttered my way over the sentence: "Where are we to put the limit between the body and the world, since the world is flesh?"

*

Body as world; world as flesh. To see the body as action, object, volume, weight, a thing that shifts, presses upon, accumulates. To consider the self tension, enactment, positive and negative space. The body: implement and receptacle. Mark maker. Mark taker. Speaker of strange, slippery language.

*

Years after getting my tattoos, I interned for a literary conference in Kenya, during which I spent a week on the Maasai Mara. One day, walking back from a Maasai settlement with Joshua and Masago, they asked about my tattoos: How were they made? How long would they last? To the latter question, I replied: "Until I die." That evening, speaking with Joshua and Masago in Maasai, Simon, a settlement chief, turned to me: "Is it true? They say your tattoos will last until death. That only then will they leave the body and enter the soil."

And the Lord Spake unto the Fish

According to dissection reports, polar bears, moose, endangered European eels, squid beaks, nine metres of rope, trash bags, two hosepipes, flowerpots, surgical gloves, a roll of duct tape, cigarette butts, sweatpants, and a golf ball have all followed Jonah into the bellies of whales.

In 1554, the French physician Guillaume Rondelet published his *Libri de piscibus marinis*. Rondelet describes the recovery of an entire suit of armour from the stomach of a shark. Rondelet postulated that it was this great fish, not a whale, that swallowed Jonah.

In this case, Jonah would have been followed over the years by a reindeer, the severed head of a horse, a Senegalese drum, one bottle of Portuguese Madeira, a bulldog on a lead, several unopened cans of salmon, a sixteenth-century Portuguese medallion worn by sailors for good fortune, a cannon ball, a chicken coop, a fur coat, one bag of semidigested banknotes, and a video camera.

Last Night, the Moon Flooded the Bedclothes

LXXIX.   Wind tore across the backyards, threw open garage doors. I sat up in bed, my hands dripping a silver that burnt violet.

LXXX.   "I have ascertained that there is a village in Lycia between Myra and Phellus called Sura where there are those who devote themselves to divination by means of fish, and they understand what it purports if the fish come at their call or withdraw, and what it signifies if they pay no attention, and what it portends if they come in numbers. And you shall hear these prophetic utterances of the sages when a fish leaps out of the water or comes floating up from the depths, and when it accepts the food or on the other hand rejects it."

—Claudius Aelian, "Divination by Fishes,"
On the Nature of Animals

LXXXI.   Pennsylvania Exhibit, St. Louis World's Fair, USA, 1904: A tunnel. The flicker of weak bulbs over glass. Fish tanks groan along the walls, their water turbid, swirling sediment. A catfish circles sluggishly. Trout, minnows, striped bass—some still gulp at the surface, the others simply float, bodies pale, bloated.

LXXXII.   The state of Pennsylvania created a tunnelled aquarium as part of its *Fish and Fisheries* exhibit at the 1904 St. Louis World's Fair, an exhibit that would inspire one of America's first aquariums, at Fairmount Park, Philadelphia. Dubbed the "grotto," this dark corridor, lined in glass jewel boxes and thirty-five fish tanks, drew some of the largest crowds of the entire fair— even if the fish often spent longer dead than alive.

LXXXIII.   Shunted some nine hundred miles by freight train from Pennsylvania to Missouri, only to be placed in excessively warm, dirty water, the fish died within days. Curators attempted to rectify the dirtiness by shovelling lime into the tanks, a measure that only increased the mortality rate. Even after efforts to filter the water's heavy aluminium content, the tanks remained far too warm and a second carload of fish, shipped overnight, began to die from fungal infections. The surviving fish received salt baths twice daily to combat infection, though this merely prolonged their life by a few days. Only months later, after a water refrigeration system was installed, did the situation improve. A third freight car arrived: fish once wild, twisting with the current of rivers, now boxed behind glass, scales shimmering in artificial light.

LXXXIV.   Thirty years of visiting tanks. Each time, they feel more forced, more aggressive. These delicate animals, once oracles of the gods, now used to pacify toddlers in the muggy, storming heat. Faces pressed to Plexiglass, camera flash, handprints, small fists pounding the acrylic. What must they think, these fish? Who is listening as they whisper blessings, cautions, messages of grace?

LXXXV.   When I think of aquariums, I remember the whirr as the escalator carried me, seven years old, through Florida's SeaWorld. Even back in 1996, it towered immense, more palace than tank. I felt I was ascending, in the divine sense, that this must be what death looked like. Only, the tanks would be open seas, Neptune arcing them into glassy vault. I remember, decades later, Toronto's case of anemones—rippling soft tendrils. The gleaming, surreal colour. The overcrowded tank of sturgeon in Tbilisi's fish market, snouts crushed against the glass. The moray eel in a Miami barbershop that jittered, distressed, every time the radio blasted through the shop.

LXXXVI.   Aquariums attract and repulse me. The dirty, cramped tanks—old aquariums still holding out. The glass metropolises of new builds, caverns of concrete, coral, fake rock. The endless Beanie toys and graphic tees: *JOIN THE SHARK SIDE, JUST A RAY OF SUNSHINE, DON'T BE JELLY*. The shadow, the power of a shark propelling overhead. The sweep of a manta ray, colossal, ancient, engulfing. And, then, the Tannoy system, the display stands of stuffed toys, the rolls of posters, the so-called huge tanks—clearly nowhere near the size of an ocean, lake, or riverbed. Plastic, acrylic, ultraviolet light. Yet there—always there, the luminosity, the blue-green glow. The slip of fishes. Everywhere the softness, the generosity of bodies that don't ask anything beyond one's capacity to give.

LXXXVII.   "They say that Pythagoras bought a draught of fishes, and presently commanded the fishers to let them all out of the net; and this shows that he did not hate or not mind fishes, as things of another kind and destructive to man, but that they were his dearly beloved creatures, since he paid a ransom for their freedom."

—Plutarch, "Why the Pythagoreans Command Fish Not to Be Eaten, More Strictly Than Other Animals," *Quaestiones convivales*

LXXXVIII.   Almost two millennia after Hiero II ordered his gargantuan ship and 1,500 years after eels wore earrings, eighteen years after the Jiajing emperor ordered his 680 fishbowls, but still three centuries before Villepreux-Power would invent the aquaria proper and four centuries before Pennsylvania's exhibit in the St. Louis World's Fair, the Swiss goldsmith, alchemist, self-taught physician, and all-round charlatan businessman Leonhard Thurneysser commissioned a Grimnitz glassblower to create a double-globe tank. Thus, in 1572, a small bowl was blown within a larger bowl. As a bird sat in the inner sphere, fish swam within the water of the larger one.

LXXXIX. This creation of birdcage within fishbowl, of doubled confinement for human leisure, figures not only in histories of the aquarium, but also in those of the paperweight and snow globe. It even gave rise to a short craze for these bird-within-fish-bowls. From 1825 to 1840, Biedermeier art glass produced examples painted in gold, transparent enamel, black enamel, and minutely decorated in seascapes. Given the creation's prominence in contemporary narratives of glass-based ornaments, one might wrongly conclude that it marked an important event for Thurneysser himself. Then, again, all is relative.

XC. What's a birdcage within a fishbowl when one has evaded capture for selling gilded lead as gold; published copious academic tracts in several languages that one neither speaks nor reads—texts that, as one's contemporaries point out, are littered with profanities and fictitious citations; when one has been appointed court physician to Johann Georg, elector of Brandenburg, after miraculously curing the latter's wife; when one subsequently sets up a urine-testing postal service, accumulating vast wealth, all whilst overseeing the court's botanical and exotic animal collections? Amidst these events, Thurneysser commissioned the birdcage within a fishbowl. The act occupies but one line in the biography of a man who, even after all these exploits, still went on to purchase land so that he might refashion himself Leonhard Thurneysser zum Thurn. A man who, upon returning to his hometown of Basel, then wildly prosperous, had a series of stained-glass windows made for his own home, in which he stood likened to Homer—a gesture that grated with the local burghers. A man who eventually lost his fortune, travelled to Italy in patronage to the Medici family, and died penniless in the house of a goldsmith—Thurneysser's original and destined trade.

XCI. Histories of the aquarium tend to focus on nineteenth-century developments up to the present day. In part, this is logical: aquariums, as we know them—large glass tanks on public display—can be traced easily from their beginnings in the parlour-room collections of nineteenth-century naturalists to their developments in zoos, fish houses, and the world exhibits of the Industrial Revolution. In such narratives, the evolution of glass tank technologies couples with the societal vogue for scientific observation and economic expansion: the aquarium is a scientific triumph and commercial venture. Even now, aquariums favour scientific narratives, highlighting their ongoing involvement in scientific observation, conservation, and repopulation even when aquariums have historically contributed to those same population deficits.

XCII. To assert that aquariums are all logic and scientific endeavour rings false. Where is the tyrannical whim for a ship the size of cities? The personal taste for 680 flower-printed basins? Economically remodelled samurai killers? Why is no one requesting a dialogue—gelatinous, coiling, electric—with the gods? And what of utter happenstance? The one-line moments in an entirely disjointed life? Thurneysser: this man who, in no way, cared for fish rearing, whom history blessed as forefather to the snow globe, to absurd kitsch, a man considered a quirk, if mentioned at all, in the lineage of aquariums. A man who requested a double-blown goldfish bowl as trinket, distraction, small folly to pass a drab week. I have never enjoyed clean history, neat lines and traceable cause and effect. I've always enjoyed a more haphazard, more crustacean zigzag through the past. I like knowing that, alongside oracular eels, Claudius Aelian documented rumours of prophetic crocodiles in ancient Egypt, crocodiles so gifted that when a forebearer of Ptolemy went to feed them, they rejected anything from his hand—a forewarning of death that came but weeks later. To know that a contemporary, secular society might scoff at the oracular fishes of the ancient Greeks, yet entrusted an octopus at the Sea Life Centre in Oberhausen, Germany, to predict the scores of international football matches, gambled hard-earned cash on the movement of a tentacle from 2008 until the creature's death in 2010. To know that Emperor Jiajing, on a separate occasion from his annual fishbowl request, ordered ten mao hsüeh p'an, or dishes for the hair and blood of sacrificial victims. That this same emperor's wives mounted an assassination attempt against him, strangling him with the ribbons in their hair, because he insisted on drinking their menstrual blood as an "elixir of life." That he had his wives executed by a thousand cuts.

XCIII.   Thurneysser illuminates something important about aquariums and their specific place in my instinctual response. The man, the snow globe—entities of contained chaos—they hint at the artifice of neat history, particularly the scientifically logical and justified one of aquariums, somewhat saturated with typically nineteenth-century evolutionary consequence and rationale. The tank itself—this desire to contain, make

neat, understand that which represents the unfathomable, the limits of human knowledge and ability. Its
inherent yet alluring violence—azure, otherworldly
incandescence. Perhaps, history should be rethought:
upended, blizzarding, fraught connections—sparking,
then lost.

XCIV. For me, fish inspire the otherworldly over scientific logic or economic gain. Fish have always swum
me beyond my body, exploded me into some other
mythic, imagined space. A state where I can breathe
easier, articulate a body that comes to me as vessel for
a soul—my soul—whose past selves I can only touch
at, not remember.

XCV. To see fish dive, dart, glide, or thrash from sight—
they dissolve hard knowledge, shimmer possibility.
In the way they suck and bury in the sand, skim the
edges of the human realm, in the way fish circle out
of reach, at depth—peripheral, liminal—they remind
me that human laws are fallible, transitory, subjugated
to this Earth and the sway of its oceans. That humanity represents but short trajectory in a world that
waits, endures its violence with patient heartbeat.

Tongue Stones

"Glossopetra, which resembles the human tongue, is not engendered, it is said, in the earth, but falls from the heavens during the moon's eclipse."

—Pliny the Elder, *Naturalis historia*

When fossilised shark teeth were first discovered embedded within rocks, no one could explain their origin, referring to them as *glossopetrae* or "tongue stones" for their unusual shape. By the Middle Ages, tongue stones were no longer believed to fall from the sky. Instead, they were considered petrified snake tongues dating to when Saint Paul, shipwrecked upon Maltese shores in AD 60, cursed all the island's serpents after a viper bit his arm. In Malta, legend was divided: some thought the shores awash with snake tongues, but others maintained it was Saint Paul's own tongue reproducing within the rock—the enduring emblem of a powerful preacher.

From the Middle Ages through to the Renaissance, *glossopetrae* were sold in abundance and continued to be traded into the early twentieth century. Carried, worn as amulets, or sewn into pockets, tongue stones protected against snakebites and poisonings. If touched upon the site of a bite or dipped into a suspect chalice, the tongue stone absolved all noxious substances. Indeed, their curative powers were such that they were employed against plagues, fevers, poxes, birthing pains, spasms, and bad breath.

In 1666, Italian fishermen towed a great white shark ashore at the port of Leghorn, now known as Livorno—the first shark catch ever registered in Tyrrhenian Sea records. After acquiring the animal's head, the Florentine Medici bequeathed the find to Niels Stenson, also known as Nicolas Steno (1638–1686), so that he might dissect it.

Three years later, Stenson published his findings. He proposed that tongue stones were the fossilised remains of shark teeth from previous geological eras—a premise that inaugurated a new science of Earth's history. Where popular belief once dated Earth at a few thousand years—its land formations unchanged since the Creation—the world suddenly aged, its soils, rocks, water, all now bore the signs of ancient decomposition and regeneration.

Yet, in 1667, far from refuting the existence of a divine hand, Stenson converted to Catholicism and was ordained titular bishop of Titiopolis a decade later. Hailed as the founder of geology and palaeontology, Stenson preached not only of Catholicism to the secular, but of science to the Church, as fierce a tongue as any saint, as double-edged as any serpent.

I Am Poured Out Like Water

According to the Puerto Rican tradition of la Noche de San Juan, those seeking protection from the island's patron saint—John the Baptist—must immerse themselves in water within the first moments of his feast day. Thus, as night descends on June 23, inhabitants gather near bodies of water: oceans, rivers, lakes, even swimming pools, or, in the case of Puerto Ricans celebrating in New York City's East River Park, buckets of water hoisted from the waterway. At midnight, as June 23 washes into June 24, those assembled wade backwards into the water, dive three, seven, some insist twelve times, but always with eyes locked, not on the sea, but on the shoreline.

It is said of la Noche de San Juan that, as you dive, you must speak to the water, relinquish your fears and regrets. You are to ask for benediction, that sickness be replaced with health, weakness with strength, you are to trust the waters will wash you out of one body and into the next.

*

Lifeguard training, North Sea, UK: Grey sky bled into grey water, snow coughed into foam, salt. An hour earlier, it had taken two men to close the zip on the wet suit I'd been given to train in.

"It's three sizes too small; this isn't going to work. I can't breathe."

"Sure it will. Besides, that's all we've got. Get in there."

In addition to the wet suit, I wore a swimsuit, rash vest, wet suit hood, shoes, and mittens—necessary insulation, fatal extra weight.

Each day that week, an unemployed former Olympic swimmer, a laid-off firefighter, a seasonal worker, and I performed rescue manoeuvres for several hours, our bodies blurring in darkness more than daylight. In need of work, we were training as beach lifeguards off-season, hoping to get on the payroll earlier come springtime. That day, there'd been a mix-up with the wet suits. I had a choice: four hours in basic swimwear in near-zero temperatures or the wrong-sized suit. I'd asked about sitting out that day—"You sit out, you go home."

I swam, my stroke blunted, four hundred yards into the chop. The suit absorbed water, grew heavier, more cumbersome with each stroke. My breath came shallow, ragged. Far out, the wind picked up, and the waves followed, snarling. My vision swam, my thoughts—dull flotsam. Oxygen deprived, I managed a single thought: remove the wet suit. I tugged at the Velcro fastenings, at the zip's pull cord.

Upon entering 4.5–10°C (40–50°F) water without insulated clothing, the human body has five minutes before it loses dexterity, thirty to sixty minutes before exhaustion or unconsciousness, and a maximum survival time of one to three hours.

Since adolescence, I've swum every morning—lap pools, rivers, lakes, seas. It's not that I had never encountered difficulty in open water before—I'd seen strong currents, freak tides, abandoned sharp objects, near-freezing temperatures—but I'd always felt a degree of control. Even when cutting it fine, my body obeyed enough, always enough to drag myself onto land, gasping, bleeding, vomiting maybe, but alive and out of danger.

That day, snow driving into the water, my lungs searing, my body blue-tinged and shaking, that day was different. For the first time, my body couldn't complete basic tasks. I understood: cold water obliterates. I couldn't free the wet suit cord. I tugged off a mitten. My hand had cramped, petrified, bruising purple-slate. I tried again. The zip snagged on the rash vest. I heaved at the zip, my body devoid of sensation beyond my chest. Fingers, hands, feet, arms, legs—I couldn't feel them, except for an occasional wave of cramping, excess weight. My body gave out, hail needling my face. I thought of the effort it had taken to get me to that point—the years of swimming, studying, of exams and low-paying temp jobs, always a hum of exhaustion, this desperation to get on, wash up somewhere quieter, rest.

The sky lurched. Waves rolled me high, plunged. Water roared, turned static as it filled my ears. The undertow—coruscant, careening, exquisite. Burning. Panic. Nausea. I swallowed water. The pain receded. A few single bubbles—large, rippling medusae—escaped my nose and mouth.

I thought, *So, this is how it goes*, my body relaxing, only wishing I could be drowning without all this gear, my body limbs free, drifting.

Which is when I was yanked upwards, a float jammed under my torso: "Hold the fuck on to that, will you."

Noise thundered back. I choked—acid, air. The water surged. My thoughts exploded into the sky, sank, churned sand and salt.

On the shore, the man—the seasonal worker training with me— told me to vomit. I gestured at the wet suit zip. After wrenching repeatedly, he pulled it loose. My body shuddered onto its hands and knees.

We were only alone a few minutes before one of the trainers came over: "What's going on? We didn't tell you to get out."

"The wet suit," I gestured at the suit, "little tight."

"So, why are there two of you?"

"Offered to help with the zip, did a tow-in rescue for the practice."

The trainer stared at us, at the vomit: "So, there's no issue here?"

I shook my head: "I'll need a larger suit tomorrow."

That day, after some ten minutes to recover my breath, I got back in the water—wet suit unzipped—and finished the exercises. For the rest of the week, I did the same—I returned to the water.

This event strangely never gave me a fear of drowning, of losing myself to water. I would take water over collision, over concrete, metal, drought, excess heat. I have always loved the roar of wild water, colossal beast. Maybe one day it will devour me, maybe that will be my time, my place—so be it.

I once met a former competitive swimmer. In her youth, she lost all her front teeth to a diving accident—started a race too deep, slammed face-first into the pool floor, blood shattering across tiles, clouding into blue. She shrugged it off: "It was an old pool, some unusual angle to the floor. They closed it not long after." She finished her drink: "All part of the job. Water can't always give. It has to take something for its time."

*

Born to the Abia priest Zechariah—a man struck dumb for doubting the prophecy of his son's birth—Saint John the Baptist spent much of his early ministry wandering the mountains of Judea in a camel-hair shift, living off locusts and raw honey. In Christian worship, he is venerated for announcing Jesus's coming and later baptising him in the River Jordan—an event that supposedly split the heavens, light pouring over algae, slow-moving catfish.

As it happens, after flowing through arid landscape for 223 miles, the River Jordan empties into the Dead Sea—one of the world's saltiest bodies of water and long frequented as a site of healing. Prized for their rejuvenating properties, its waters are paradoxically devoid of life, nine times saltier than seawater, and dense enough that the human body floats upon their surface.

During the first century BC, Herod I, king of Judea, and his son Herod Antipas bathed in the Dead Sea. Two of the Dead Sea's most prominent patrons to date, the first was mythologized for ordering the Massacre of the Innocents, the second—for delivering Saint John the Baptist's head upon a silver platter.

And so to strange confluence: Saint John the Baptist would begin and end his ministry within the course of a single river—baptise the Son of God in its body, lose his life at its mouth.

*

"Water is also a *type of destiny*. . . . One cannot bathe twice in the same river because already, in his inmost recesses, the human being shares the destiny of flowing water. Water is truly the transitory element. . . . A being dedicated to water is a being in flux. He dies every minute; something of his substance is constantly falling away. . . . Daily death is the death of water. Water always flows, always falls, always ends in horizontal death."

—Gaston Bachelard, *Water and Dreams: An Essay on*
the Imagination of Matter

*

Celtic Sea, UK: Dawn. The water crested, exploded vaporous over my face. I pushed out further, beyond the strands of bladder wrack, beyond the throw of high breakers, swam to where the waves still gathered momentum, slow roll and swell, low growl as the sea awoke. Terns rose and sank through the mist. The shoreline smudged from sight. As I floated on my back, a gull sliced through the sea mist, its wings almost brushing my rib cage, and settled unnaturally close.

Caws. Wingbeats. Feathers. Five gulls settled within arm's reach. And they stayed there, in the bitter cold, spume whipping between our bodies, carried on an offshore wind. All the while, they floated next to me, these creatures of open water. Guardians with wings of granite, gale, and storm.

*

Winding through the Jordan Rift Valley, the River Jordan has the lowest elevation of any river on Earth, its banks, at times, soaring 3,000 feet above its waters. As the river progresses toward the Dead Sea, it drops further, sinking into a body of water 1,410 feet below sea level, which is to say the lowest point on Earth's surface.

*

In 1964, Israel inaugurated its National Water Carrier, diverting water from the Sea of Galilee for national usage. In the three years that ensued, Israel, Egypt (then known as the United Arab Republic), Jordan, Syria, Iraq, and Lebanon became locked in what is referred to as the War over Water, culminating in the Six-Day War of 1967. In the decade that followed, Jordan and Syria began a simultaneous water diversion project, draining water from the Yarmuk River. Since the 1960s, the Dead Sea receives barely 10 percent of the yearly water supply required to maintain its size. Spanning fifty miles across in the 1950s, it measured only thirty miles across in 2005. With waters receding at a rate of three feet per year and sinkholes littering its periphery, the Dead Sea is, by general consensus, dying.

*

"Some say that it bears up only Live things, and lets things Inanimate sink to the Bottom; nay, that if a lighted Candle be plunged into it, it will float above, But if put out, it will sink to the bottom. . . . They say

that there are Apple-Trees upon the sides of this Sea, which bear very
lovely Fruit, but within are all full of Ashes."

—Jean de Thévenot, "Of the Dead-Sea," *The Travels of
Monsieur de Thévenot into the Levant in Three Parts*

*

I have chosen universities, jobs, and apartments based around their
proximity to swimming pools. When I can't swim, my skin comes
up in rashes, my stomach cramps, my thoughts fall leaden.

The months before that dawn swim in the Celtic Sea were the
months when I tore the muscles down my back, the months when
my mind shattered, the months when doctors told me I would never
swim again.

*

Baptism, bird dealers, converts, cutters, epileptics, farriers,
Freemasons, innkeepers, Jordan, lambs, monastic life, motorways,
oars, printers, Puerto Rico, tailors, Knights Hospitaller, Knights of
Malta, Maltese Knights, Worshipful Company of Tallow Chandlers,
as well as invocations against spasms, epilepsy, and hailstorms are
counted amongst Saint John the Baptist's patronages.

*

After months of physiotherapy and dieticians, of eventual, slow convalescence, my family took me on holiday. At the time, I couldn't
think of anything worse. But it was this trip that brought me to the
Celtic Sea, that brought me back to water. It was during this week
that I found myself on my back, a sea haar rolling over my limbs, gulls
floating beside me, early one morning off England's southwest coast.

Since the back injury, I'd kept strange hours—heavy medications
disrupted my sleep, my thoughts tended to flood at night. I suffered

from insomnia, and, if I did sleep, I had nightmares, night sweats. That week, I slept a few hours in the early morning, woke around 4:30 a.m., the hotel bedsheets damp. I boiled the kettle and watched the waves crash ink-black to slate-blue through the window.

Once a traditional 1930s British coastal hotel, the building had undergone a renovation—new carpets, wallpaper, curtains— but certain features remained: the tight rooms, narrow bathrooms, and windows that opened past safety-certified heights. One morning, as the dawn light broke over the shoreline, washed its way up the cliff into my room, I reached into my bag—my swim gear still there, untouched. I'd never unpacked it, even a year later.

I opened the ground-floor window and stepped onto the grassy clifftop, the last gusts of a night gale tearing at my T-shirt. I walked around the hotel to its terrace, where I found the establishment's original beach access: a series of steps cut into the rock face decades earlier. Disused, narrow, alternately crusted in barnacles and slicked in gutweed, the steps ended in an explosion of rocks—a section of the cove that caused the sea to thrash at high tide, spray arcing above the cliff. Sliding down the steps in a seated position, the sea-weed too thick and slippery for anything else, I breathed deeper, salt and darkness filling my mouth. At the bottom, I removed my train-ers, the only pair I'd brought, and started crossing the rocks bare-foot. My shorts clung to my legs, sodden, muddied, mucus-streaked from the clumps of purplish carragheen. I crawled between rock pools. Limpets pressed into my stomach. Sand hoppers flickered around my forearms. Barnacles sliced my feet. I no longer cared, simply kept on until I reached the shoreline. Treading blood across the sand, I removed my shorts and T-shirt. Wind bit up and down the cove. I en-tered the water, let the waves drag me into numbing, barrelling tide.

*

Water constitutes 60 percent of the human body, of which the brain and heart are 73 percent water, the lungs—83 percent, the skin—

64 percent, the muscles and kidneys—79 percent, and the skeletal structure—dry, chalky thing—a third aqueous.

Most saltwater fishes guard against the salinity of surrounding water by excreting sodium in large quantities. The fish's internal organs maintain disequilibrium between low-sodium body and saline world. Sharks and rays, however, equalise levels of water salinity, their flesh as salty as the waters in which they swim. The human body, by contrast, has not evolved such mechanisms to guard against high saline concentrations.

*

On November 15, 2016, twenty-five swimmers from diverse nations embarked upon an eleven-mile, seven-hour, and previously unattempted swim across the Dead Sea in an effort to raise awareness of its ecological decline. Owing to the Dead Sea's exceptionally high salt concentration, participants faced a twofold challenge: one, swimming in water so buoyant as to render leg movement near impossible; and, two, retaining sufficient levels of bodily hydration as the sea leached water from their bodies.

Talking of the lake's salinity, one of the swim's organisers, Uri Sela, remarked, "Swallowing one cup of this water is equivalent to a viper bite in terms of damage to the nervous system, and that's why there are more drownings in the Dead Sea than in the Mediterranean." Wearing a specially designed snorkel and mask that encased the entire face, swimmers stopped every half hour to drink and every hour to eat. At each break, the swimmers were doused in freshwater to counteract the excretion of fluids through their skin. During the swim, four participants required periods of rest on the medical vessel, one of whom—the sixty-one-year-old Palestinian lifeguard Yussuf Matari—recovered in the shade of the boat's tarp whilst hooked up to an IV before returning to the waters. Three swimmers failed to finish.

When interviewed at the finish line, participants discussed the challenges of swimming in hypersaline water—the buoyancy, the dehydration—but it was a less-anticipated factor that emerged as their greatest cause for discomfort: extensive chafing. The salt was so dense, and the bodily abrasion so great, that for seven hours swimmers experienced a sensation not of water, but of burning.

*

A dead sea dying. A preservation effort by way of swimming in water trying to kill you. Perhaps it is not so strange that baptism should eventually carry into lifeless salinity, one man's ministry—into slaughter. From the asphalt once mined to embalm Egyptian mummies to the potash now employed in modern-day fertilizers, from its waters proving toxic to their being a source of healing and vitality, the Dead Sea has always occupied a contradictory position between preservation and revivification, has always existed at the threshold of the holy, the medicinal, and the dead.

*

That morning, my mind a dull percussion as I floated on the Celtic Sea, the water returned a part of myself I had liked, had known and claimed as defining. I remembered, quite simply: I liked swimming. The physicality, the rite and ritual of moving a body through water. Swimming brought me back to myself, decades-old anchor to my sense of who I was and how I did. I remembered what it felt like to connect, to feel, to physically take part in a call and answer with the world.

I stayed with the sky and the gulls until my hands cramped, at which point I began a slow swim back, aided by the waves that, despite the outward tide, raged for the shoreline. I took a hit towards the beach. A wave pulled me under, dragged my body against the bottom. I staggered from the sea. An early-morning dog walker rushed over at the sight of me: a face full of sand, grit, dripping blood.

After telling an absolutely bewildered woman that, *no, I didn't re-*
quire assistance, I felt better than I had in months, well, no, not the
face, nor the whiplash in the neck, those would take some days to heal
up, but, otherwise, yes, I was fine, thanks, I recovered my sopping,
sand-streaked shorts and T-shirt, clambered gingerly over rocks,
picked up my thankfully still dry trainers, climbed the steps, and
eventually burst—to the horror of every well-dressed breakfasting
guest—through the terrace French doors. A bluish-white slab of a
body, wearing nothing but a faded swimsuit, I staggered between
the tables, sluiced water, seaweed, and blood over chinaware as I
made my way into the lobby and up the stairs.

*

One tends to think of baptism as a miraculous instant, of its imagery as purified—scenes of cherubim, nibbling fishes, hovering white
doves. But what if baptism takes a year, decades, a lifetime? We
are talking of immense bodies, scaled creatures slinking through
the deep, of Saint John the Baptist, a transition between Old and
New Testament—watery, tenuous, calm surface to an ancient tur-
bulence. What if baptism is as old, as ongoing, and as unpredictable
as the waters that bear the blessing?

*

"I am poured out like water; all my bones are out of joint."
                    —Psalms 22:14, International Standard Version

*

In 1947, three Bedouin shepherds, Muhammed edh-Dhib, Jum'a
Muhammed, and Khalil Musa, were searching for a stray goat in
the Judean desert when edh-Dhib fell into a cave chamber and discovered clay jars housing ancient scrolls. Located at Qumran, on the

northern shore of the Dead Sea, this would be the first of a series of cave chambers, eventually excavated in 1949. After passing through the hands of antiques dealers and, later, scholars, the scrolls, re-named the Dead Sea Scrolls, would be dated between the last three centuries BC and the first century AD—the second-oldest manu-scripts to be included in the Hebrew Bible canon.

Amongst the fragments that make up the Dead Sea Scrolls, there exists one entitled "A Baptismal Liturgy," of which the last verse proclaims: "For You made me. . . . Your will is that we cleanse ourselves. . . . His people in the waters of bathing (. . .) second time upon his station. And he shall say in response: *'Blessed are You. (. . .) Your purification in Your glory (. . .) eternally. And today (. . .)'*"

*

"During that time, all the *Greeks, Cophtes, Armenians,* &c. Performed their Devotions also; most part go into the Water stark-naked, (espe-cially the Men) and the Women in their Smocks; they had of the Water of *Jordan* poured upon their Heads, in memory of our Lords Baptism, and washed their Linen in it, carrying away Jarrs and Bottles full of Water, with Mud and Earth, which they took up by the River side, not forgetting Sticks, which they cut in the adjoining Woods, and all to be kept as Relicks."

—Jean de Thévenot, "Of the River of Jordan," The Travels of
Monsieur de Thévenot into the Levant in Three Parts

*

At present, the Catholic Church recognises the Shrine of Saint John the Baptist—located within the Umayyad Mosque, Damascus—as the official resting place of Saint John's severed head. According to the tenth-century Persian historian Ibn al-Faqih, eighth-century construction workers discovered the saint's head in a previously concealed cave-chapel when demolishing the Byzantine cathedral to make way for a mosque. Shown to the Umayyad caliph, the head was subsequently buried under a specific pillar later inlaid with marble.

But the Knights Templars in Amiens Cathedral, France, also claim to hold the skull of Saint John the Baptist. In fact, the entire cathedral was built specifically for this purpose when Wallon de Sarton returned from the fourth raid of Constantinople in 1206, allegedly with the saint's head in his possession. Discovered by Sarton in a raided palace, the skull sat atop a silver platter sealed within a crystal hemisphere. The salver bore a Greek engraving that proclaimed these to be John the Baptist's remains. Sarton carried the relic to Amiens, pawning the silver platter to pay for his passage back to France. Since its arrival in Amiens, long-standing belief has dictated that a cavity above the skull's left eye socket was inflicted when Herod Antipas's wife, Herodias, stabbed the saint. After the French Revolution of 1789, many of Amiens Cathedral's relics were confiscated. This zeal culminated in November 1793, when members of the government ordered the Amiens relics be interred in the cemetery. Risking capital punishment, the city's mayor, Louis-Alexandre Lescouvé, secretly transported John the Baptist's head to his own home. The relic shuffled from one hiding place to another until it was returned to the cathedral in 1816. The skull still rests beneath the same crystal globe as it did in 1206, but thanks to an addition in 1876, it now boasts a jewel-encrusted platter—not silver, but gold.

Such endorsements might deter some laying claim to the high-profile relic. Yet in the Basilica of San Silvestro in Capite in Rome, a skull—worn smooth by centuries of devoted hands and greening with age—rests upon red velvet. Now sheltered by a glass case and kept out of pilgrims' reach by way of a gold pedestal, the relic stands above a Latin plaque—*Caput Sti. Joannis Baptistae Draecursoris Domini*. A stained-glass window of the saint's freshly decapitated head arcs the relic as wood and marblework carvings reenact the decapitation around the chapel.

In the Munich Residenz Museum in Germany, there is also no

lack of velvet, though on this occasion the craftsmen opted for grey. Saint John the Baptist's skull sits within a velvet reliquary, itself sunk into a velvet presentation cushion. Pearls tangle, vine-like, across the fabric. A crown of enamel flowers glints red-white. In this instance, Saint John the Baptist's head was recovered by Duke Wilhelm V of Bavaria, or his son Maximilian I, after Pope Paul IV granted Wilhelm V the right to collect relics in 1557 during the Counter-Reformation. Many of the relics housed in the Munich Residenz are now thought to have originated from exhumed Roman catacombs, bones from the unknown, but very much disturbed, dead.

In addition to his head existing in four locations, John the Baptist's right hand, with which he baptised Jesus, can be found in the Serbian Orthodox Cetinje Monastery in Montenegro, the Topkapi Palace in Istanbul, and in the Romanian Skete of the Forerunner on Mount Athos. The saint's left—and less revered—hand is apparently housed in just a single location—the Armenian Apostolic Church of Saint John at Chinsurah, West Bengal.

*

The Bedouin sold many of the Dead Sea scroll fragments to the Bethlehem antiques dealer Khalil Iskandar Shahin in the 1950s. The sale of these fragments worldwide lasted into the 1960s and 1970s. But with the passing of a UNESCO convention on cultural property and an Israeli law pertaining to the antiquities trade, only those scroll fragments that had already entered the private market could be traded.

The sale of Dead Sea scroll fragments had all but evaporated until 2002, when collectors began unveiling coin-sized pieces of parchment supposedly originating from a collection previously secreted by Khalil Iskandar Shahin in a Swiss vault. Within ten years, seventy such artefacts had entered the market.

The Museum of the Bible in Washington, D.C., USA, holds sixteen fragments purchased from the 2002 wave. In March 2020, the museum published findings that the entirety of their core collection was, in fact, fake.

Housed in the Israel Museum's Shrine of the Book exhibit in Jerusalem, the original and genuine fragments are all made from lightly tanned parchment, whereas fifteen of the sixteen fragments in Washington are made from ancient leather, most likely recovered from the Judean desert in the form of a Roman-era shoe or sandal. Researchers calculated that forgers treated the leather with animal glue before inking characters across the surface.

Once believed the oldest of biblical texts, these forgeries have become strange objects. No longer embodying the sacred, but the fraudulent, they are now widely considered worthless. And yet, as forgeries, the fragments speak to humanity's enduring desire to believe, to witness the divine on Earth, even in the face of improbable odds. In this sense, they have switched function, transformed from artefacts into spurious but treasured relics.

*

I have always felt less alone in water. As if it knows me, somehow. As if all water, wherever it may be—pool, lake, river, or sea—is connected, recognises, remembers, welcomes us back. Each morning, I talk to the water, lay desires, doubts, lay fears into its current. I wish I could better thank water. If gratitude could have dimensions, if I could cast it into the swell—an anchor point for shimmering bodies, fronded life. Instead, each morning, I throw myself.

*

Sometimes the events of one's life—their meaning, gravity, their respective weight—don't correspond to the dictates of conventional belief. When I think of dying at sea, I think of that morning amidst the gulls, not the day I nearly drowned.

The near-drowning was not stressful; I wasn't struggling with myself. Nor, when I consider my memories of water, does it stand out. Almost drowning was simply part of swimming, of spending so much time within water—a barter I've always accepted. But that year of illness—slowly wheezing on floors, my body aching across mattresses—somewhere along the line, I lost myself. Whoever I had been, whatever former sense of self I considered mine—it sank until I didn't know how to get it back. By the time I was floating on the Celtic Sea, surrounded by gulls and the burr of dawn light through the mist, I'm not sure I quite qualified as alive. One thing's for sure: if ever there has been a baptism in my life—that was it.

At the time, I didn't see it as a death or a beginning, though it was. I came to that water as chunk meat. And the water, colossal beast, carried me, washed me, and spat me—bloodied, resuscitated—onto the shoreline.

*

"In water everything is 'dissolved,' every 'form' is broken up, everything that has happened ceases to exist; nothing that was before remains after immersion in water, not an outline, not a 'sign,' not an 'event.' Immersion is the equivalent, at the human level, of death, and at the cosmic level, of the cataclysm (the Flood) which periodically dissolves the world into the primeval ocean. Breaking up all forms, doing away with all the past, water possesses this power of purifying, of regenerating, of giving new birth; for what is immersed in it 'dies,' and, rising again from the water, is . . . able to receive a new revelation and begin a new and *real* life. . . . Water purifies and regenerates because it nullifies the past, and restores—even if only for a moment—the integrity of the dawn of things."

—Mircea Eliade, *Patterns in Comparative Religion*

*

Baptism—to be reborn through water. In other words, to die and rise. Wash a body with new life. Whether understood metaphorically— to break from and renew oneself—or literally—a body divinely drowned, reanimated into different self—to baptise is always, in some sense, to multiply, to disperse oneself.

Each time I enter water, I pray that I might slough weight, those parts of myself that chafe, that come to this world, to another, as small, ungenerous. I pray for the slow erosion of water, for its tumultuous break. That this body might reveal itself soft green to grey, barnacled, slipping in lampreys, pulsing anemones, bull kelp, a thing of occasional phosphorescence, that tides, regenerates.

Last Night, Eels Crashed from the Faucet

XCVI.   A single bulb burned above the bathtub—wet, glittering.
Light snaked, smeared ceramic.
Bathe, Lars, just bathe.

XCVII. "Eels rub against rocks and the scrapings come to life; this is their only way of breeding."
—Pliny the Elder, *Naturalis historia*

XCVIII. According to ancient Egyptian theology, Atum is the god of gods. Emerging from the first waters of chaos, he spat the gods from his mouth as humans emerged from his eyes. An alternative myth maintains that Atum was created by the Eight Gods, or Ogdoad. Either way, Atum would eventually destroy the world, sink it beneath primal waters, and take the form of a snake. Serpents were attributed to Atum. But so was one other animal: the eel.

XCIX.   In Naukratis, Egypt, votive boxes to Atum were discovered carved in the shape of sacred reptiles, each containing the corresponding mummified animal remains. Of the ninety-four votive boxes recovered, the majority understandably included snakes and lizards, yet thirteen of the boxes contained mummified eels.

C.   Atlanta, Georgia, USA, 2019: In the Georgia Aquarium that day, the outside world blurring in sticky heat, storms, sheet rain, I watched a fire eel sift between pearl gourami, greater scissortails, between hillstream loaches or, as they are otherwise known—"lizardfish." Slate grey, body scorched in red stripes, the fire eel can grow beyond four feet in the wild. In captivity, even when housed in the largest aquaria, fire eels do not grow beyond twenty-two inches, nor do they reproduce. Predominantly found in Cambodia, Indonesia, Laos, Malaysia, Thailand, and Vietnam, the fire eel prefers brackish water and a sand bed in which to bury itself—often entirely, save its snout. Aquarium guides recommend keeping fire eels alone in large tanks to curb their aggression, which is to say: to prevent them hunting. It is likewise noted that the water need not be brackish, the gravel not too deep, and that plants should be attached to rocks to prevent the eel uprooting foliage when burying. In the aquarium trade, fire eels are sourced by dry-pumping bodies of standing water, by digging the eels from rapidly parched mud beds. In the Georgia Aquarium, I watched the fire eel ribbon through fluorescent water, twitch through fronds of Myrio Green. A nocturnal hunter known for flaming through darkness, this beast of flood and furnace—now spot-lit, suspended in acrylic.

CI.   For millennia, the eel has eluded humankind. Its lifespan, morphology, migratory patterns, reproductive practices—all have slipped from grasp. Only in the past century or so has the European eel, *Anguilla anguilla*, curled into light.

CII.   Originally mistaken by philosophers, naturalists, and scientists as four separate creatures, the European eel passes through several morphological stages across its lifespan—each significantly distinct from the last. Spawning in the Sargasso Sea—a fact discovered only because Johannes Schmidt, a Danish biologist, spent nearly a decade chasing eel migratory routes— the *Anguilla anguilla* begins life as a larva, drifting off swathes of *Sargassam* weed. The American eel also uses this breeding ground, though it is still unknown how the two species' larvae, seemingly identical and intermingled in the kelp, instinctually navigate to their respective habitats on opposite sides of the Atlantic. Yet, it is here in the Sargasso Sea, a body of water bound, not by land, but by currents—the Gulf Stream, the North Atlantic Drift, the Canary Current, and the North Equatorial Current—it is here, in this twisting fever dream of a sea, that the European eel first swims into the world.

CIII.   Carried in the Gulf Stream, the larvae gradually transform into colourless glass eels or "elvers" as they reach the continental shelf. They then wriggle towards the European and North African coasts, some already morphing into their third incarnation: the yellow eel. At this point, the eel may or may not enter freshwater: some eels remain in seawater, whilst others swim upstream, unaffected by the change in salinity, even slithering across mud to reach streams, inland lakes. But the final metamorphosis of the European eel, that of the silver eel, is the most elusive, taking place at any age upwards of twenty years. Until the eel matures, it remains within a habitat of several hundred yards, growing up to seven feet, slowly filtering the slip of decades, occasionally a near century. No one understands when or why an eel decides to silver, only that when it does, it winds its way back to the sea. Turning an iridescent silver, the eel transforms: its eyes increase in size, its pectoral fin in length; its fat content increases, and its alimentation tract regresses as its reproductive organs develop.

CIV.   Silver eels, some older than humans, migrate back to the Sargasso Sea. They eat nothing, subsist solely on their accumulated body fat, and navigate by instinct, currents, water temperature—no one knows. After years, an eel returns to its water within water, mates, and dies—though no one has ever witnessed these acts either.

CV.   "Whenever the Moray is filled with amorous impulses it comes out of the sea on to land seeking eagerly for a mate, and a very evil mate. For it goes to a viper's den and the pair embrace. And they do say that the male viper also in its frenzied desire for copulation goes down to the sea, and just as a reveller with his flute knocks at the door, so the viper also with his hissing summons his loved one, and she emerges. Thus does Nature bring

those that dwell far apart together in a mutual desire
and to a common bed."

—Claudius Aelian, "The Moray and the Viper,"
On the Nature of Animals

CVI.   Prehistoric, primal: I've always felt the eel swims closer
to the gods, that it somehow writhes between realms.
More mystery than revelation. More distinct from
this world than of it. As a child, I believed eels knotted
my gut, and, still, along with the pike, eels slide into
my sleep, ripple through open windows, slither from
under the bed. Triangular jaw, short, blunt teeth, they
lie dormant, mature in the dirt and mud of this body,
days drifting into a sediment of years. If the sturgeon
swims our soul, swims distant star blast, ancient energy through this life, then eels must be the last echo
of the gods. The closest we can get to a messenger of
realms, creature of primal waters and their creators
slinking through ourselves.

CVII.   I often wonder what movement we are caught in, what,
if anything, is guiding all of us. Eddying our bodies,
churning times, places into rough chop. Sometimes,
I feel the world as rushing drive, a river emptying
scorching knowledge, tearing up the earth, coursing
through rock. Other times, I feel an evening expand,
mapped somehow onto the slower drift of seas, lan-
guorous tides. But, I guess, all eventually comes cir-
cling to reemerge as undercurrent, tide, as flood.

CVIII.   Once, when I was still only seven or so, a group of my
mother's art students took me swimming late at night
on the Aberystwyth coast. I can't remember why I
was there exactly. But I remember how they suddenly

decided, kicked off their shoes, ran in. The impulse. How one of the boys took my hand and ran with me into breakers five times my height. How he helped me dive and jump through the waves, the current immense, enraged. I remember us all—decades apart—standing there on the shore afterwards, T-shirts pulling off our bodies, seawater and moonlight streaming from our jean pockets. The pebbles glistened. I looked out, the sky an infinite black, wet almost, and the breakers—thunderous, cresting, luminescent. Searing light over dark waters—caught, dashed.

CIX.   "Remember . . . before the days of trouble come, . . . before the sun and the light and the moon and the stars are darkened and the clouds return with the rain; . . . before the silver cord is snapped, and the golden bowl is broken, and the pitcher is broken at the fountain, and the wheel broken at the cistern, and the dust returns to the earth as it was, and the breath returns to God who gave it."
        —Ecclesiastes 12:1–7, New Revised Standard Version

CX.   I stood for nearly an hour in front of the fire eel. My body simultaneously heavy, yet held—weed furring its edges. This animal—its life, its movements, all curtailed—gave me a gift I could not repay: rest, brief rest in this world. Minutes later, as I passed through a blue-lit corridor, a woman—middle-aged, *OHIO BOBCATS* ball cap, Disney sweatshirt, pink fanny pack—looked me up and down, grimaced. Walking on, I caught her husband's voice, "Children here, and we let perverts walk around."

CXI.   To feel more comfortable, ever more akin to other beasts. More aqueous than terrestrial. How common to feel completely at odds with being human? To dream, night after night, until the years tumble, crash in on themselves. To dream of waters rising, of the world roaring, submerged. Highways and tower blocks—lost and blinking, to hear the waves sweeping cars against buildings. And the animals—seabirds, sharks, the great Cetus—all older than gospel. To hear the sound of prophecy—feral, cawing. Messengers long unheeded, now unbridled as they swim the streets.

CXII. That day, stepping from the Georgia Aquarium into the growl of a thunderstorm, cars sluicing water across the pavements, the childhood photograph glowing off my phone with each notification, I thought back to the tropical storm that hit Sanibel Island during that 1990s holiday. On Sanibel, as the storm raged—five days, five nights—I watched the world flood. I wondered whether it was sinking or whether the waters were finally rising—a great foaming mouth to swallow a world I didn't understand. As if the underworld— silent, soft-shanked—had come to engulf this land of hot, frantic movement. During those days and nights, I watched fish glide between car tyres, suck at weed caught in hubcaps, their bodies illuminated by the beam of car park floodlights. Egrets fluttered from tree to tree. An alligator swam past a convenience store, its body incandescent in blue neon—*24 HOUR, BUDWEISER, CAMEL LIGHTS.*

CXIII. "They say that men have explored the sea to a depth of 300 fathoms, but not as yet beyond that. Whether there are fishes and animals swimming at an even greater depth, or whether even to them these regions are inaccessible, although the gods of the sea and also the

overlord of the moist world have their allotted dwelling
there—these are matters into which I shall not enquire
too closely, and no one else informs us.".

—Claudius Aelian, "The Depths of the Sea,"
On the Nature of Animals

CXIV.   All those years ago, I watched the world liquefy, and,
for a moment, one brief, rippling moment—it made
sense. The emptiness, the quiet—the lack of human
footfall, just the catfish, the alligators, pelicans gliding knowingly across it all. Streetlamps burnt over
dark water. I felt my body fit. Felt how this world—
obscured, glassy, teeming with hidden life—how it
resembled me, or I it. Or, maybe, it was simply a
space through which I could softly slip. Those nights,
I dreamt that I lay in the flooded tennis courts, that
my body floated past the dirty net, past the chain-
link fence, silt-smeared shopfronts, that it drifted
into the river of the street, spiralled into new movement. I dreamt that the fishes carried in the current
beside me. That the pike, eels, the sturgeon—they
swam in and out of this body, moved through this
world with ease. That, in some strange, gilled sense,
my body finally breathed.

Notes

Preface

Information pertaining to the *The Book-Fish* was found in Andrew Herd's article "Strange Things Found inside Fish," first published in *Waterlog* magazine and later reproduced for the Fisherman's Museum online, 2012.

Last Night, a Pike Swam up the Stairs

I owe initial thanks to Bernd Brunner's *The Ocean at Home: An Illustrated History of the Aquarium* (New York: Princeton Architectural Press, 2005) and Celeste Olalquiaga's *The Artificial Kingdom: A Treasury of the Kitsch Experience* (New York: Pantheon Books, 1998). These two books sparked much of my research for this extended essay in their engaging and quirky histories of aquariums.

Many of the strange facts peppered through their initial overviews went on to occupy significant time and fruitful endeavour in my own work.

The full reference of quotations from *The Deipnosophists* is as follows: Athenaeus of Naucratis, *The Deipnosophists, or Banquet of the Learned of Athenaeus*, c. AD 200–300, trans. C. D. Yonge (London: Henry G. Bohn, York Street, Covent Garden, 1854), vol. 7, pp. 487–489.

When researching fish tanks on ancient watercraft, I found Albert J. Klee's article "The Myth of the Roman Aquarium: Reflections on Aquarium Hobby History Research" most instructive (republished and available on Wet Web Media: http://www.wetwebmedia.com/MythRomanAqKlee.htm).

Details of the Fiumicino 5 wreck first appear in Giulia Boetto's "The Museum of the Roman Ships: The Port of Claudius," trans. Claire Calcagno (Rome: Soprintendenza archeologica di Ostia, Roma, 1998) (https://www2.rgzm.de/navis/musea/ostia/Fiumicino_English.htm); and Giulia Boetto's "Roman Techniques for the Transport and Conservation of Fish: The Case of the Fiumicino 5 Wreck" in *An Offprint from Connected by the Sea: Proceedings of the Tenth International Symposium on Boat and Ship Archaeology, Roskilde 2003*, eds. Lucy Blue, Fred Hocker, and Anton Englert (Oxford, UK: Oxbow Books, 2006), pp. 123–129. See also Lionel Casson's "Harbour and River Boats of Ancient Rome" in *Journal of Roman Studies* (London: Society for the Promotion of Roman Studies, 1965), vol. 55, no. 1/2, pp. 31–39.

The full reference for Pliny's remark on bejewelled eels is as follows: Pliny the Elder, *Naturalis historia*, AD 77, trans. W. H. S. Jones (Cambridge, MA: Harvard University Press, 1868–1944), vol. XXXII., chap. VII.

Thanks to the Labraunda online resource centre for its extensive reports of the archaeological digs at Labraunda (http://www.labraunda.org/Labraunda.org/Introduction_eng.html).

The full reference of the quotation taken from Claudius Aelian's *On the Nature of Animals* is: Claudius Aelian (c. AD 175–c. 235),

"Tame Fishes," in *De natura animalium* or *On the Nature of Animals*, trans. A. F. Scholfield (Cambridge, MA: Harvard University Press, 1958), vol. VIII., chap. IV.

Details of the *Turritopsis dohrnii* species of jellyfish were obtained thanks to M. P. Miglietta and H. A. Lessios, "A Silent Invasion," *Biological Invasions* (Springer, 2008), pp. 825–834.

As for the Tilapia

When researching the role of the tilapia in ancient Egypt, I consulted *The Egyptian Book of the Dead*, trans. Sir Peter Le Page Renouf and Professor E. Naville, as well as Patrick Hunt's article "Ancient Egyptian Tilapia Fish Story," *Electrum Magazine*, September 29, 2012.

Last Night, a Doctor Handed Me a Glass of Water

The full reference for the quotation from Plutarch is as follows: Plutarch, *Quaestiones convivales*, compiled in *Plutarch's Morals*, c. AD 100. Translated from the Greek by several hands, corrected and revised by William W. Goodwin (Boston: Little, Brown, 1874), vol. VIII, chap. VIII, section IV.

I am indebted to the works of Stephen W. Bushell and Anna Marie Roos for their insightful observations on Ming porcelain and Japanese traditions of goldfish breeding, namely: Stephen Wootton Bushell, William M. Laffan, D. Appleton and Company, and L. Prang & Co., *Oriental Ceramic Art: Illustrated by Examples from the Collection of W. T. Walters: With One Hundred and Sixteen Plates in Colors and over Four Hundred Reproductions in Black and White*, vol. 4 (New York: D. Appleton and Company, 1897); and Anna Marie Roos, *Goldfish* (London: Reaktion Books, 2019).

For more information concerning the Xuande fishbowl sold by Sotheby's auction house, consult "Fishes in the Imperial Pond—an Exceptional Xuande Bowl," April 5, 2017, Hong Kong. Sale number: HK0766.

The full reference for the list quoted in Bushell's work is as follows: Stephen W. Bushell, *Oriental Ceramic Art: Illustrated by Examples from the Collection of W. T. Walters*, vol. 4 (New York: D. Appleton and Company, 1897).

The Conviction of Things Not Seen

Facts pertaining to the Greenland shark were found thanks to Mark Schrope's article "Mysterious Giant Sharks May Be Everywhere," BBC Earth, October 24, 2014.

The Georgian Military Road

Statistics on the number of Georgians killed and exiled after the 1924 uprising are quoted from: David Marshall Lang, *A Modern History of Georgia* (London: Weidenfeld and Nicolson, 1962), pp. 243-244.

Information pertaining to Russia's recent LGBT legislation appears in "Concluding Observations on the Combined Fourth and Fifth Periodic Reports of the Russian Federation," Convention on the Rights of the Child, February 25, 2014.

Sources consulted when researching Vladislav Tornovoi's murder include "Arrests over 'Anti-Gay' Murder in Volgograd Russia," BBC News Europe, May 13, 2013; Alexander Winning, "Homophobic Killing Sparks Outrage," *Moscow Times*, May 12, 2013; Юлия Чернухина, "Мотив для убийства," *Новое Время*, no. 17 (285), 20 мая 2013 (https://newtimes.ru/articles/detail/66578/); Даниил Туровский, "'Стал геем, чтобы оттуда сбежать' Кто и за что убил Владислава Торнового," *Лента.ру*, 23 мая 2013 (https://lenta.ru/articles/2013/05/23/volgograd).

Sources consulted when researching Oleg Serdyuk's murder include Steve Gutterman, eds. Elizabeth Piper, Pravin Char, "Gay Man Killed in Russia's Second Suspected Hate Crime in Weeks," Reuters, June 3, 2013. Владимир Хитров, "Убийство на Камчатке:

гомофобы? быдло?" *Эхо Москвы*, 03 июня 2013 (https://echo.msk
.ru/blog/vladimir_khitrov/1087640-echo/).

For the December 29, 2014, Russian Federation road safety order,
see: http://cdnimg.rg.ru/pril/article/106/84/30/voditeli-medicina
.pdf. For the corresponding English definitions of the disorders
listed, see: International Statistical Classification of Diseases and
Related Health Problems 10th Revision (ICD-10)-WHO Version for
2016 (https://icd.who.int/browse10/2016/en#/F60-F69).

Sources consulted when researching the Chechen concentration
camps include: Елена Милашина, "Убийство чести," *Новая Газета*,
1 апреля 2017 (https://novayagazeta.ru/articles/2017/04/01/71983
-ubiystvo-chesti); Ирина Гордиенко, Елена Милашина, "Расправы
над чеченскими геями," *Новая Газета*, 4 апреля 2017 (https://
novayagazeta.ru/articles/2017/04/04/72027-raspravy-nad
-chechenskimi-geyami-publikuem-svidetelstva); Masha Gessen, "A
Damning New Report on L.G.B.T. Persecution in Chechnya," *New
Yorker*, December 21, 2018; "Chechnya LGBT: Dozens 'Detained
in New Gay Purge,'" BBC News Europe, January 14, 2019; and "2
Tortured to Death in New Anti-Gay Purge in Chechnya, Activist
Says," *Moscow Times*, January 14, 2019.

Last Night, Sturgeon Swam the Streets

The Scribonius Largus quotation originally appears in Latin in
Scribonius Largus, *Scribonii Largi conpositiones* [*sic*], ed. G. Helmreich
(Leipzig: B. G. Teubneri, 1887), p. 9. Court physician to Emperor
Claudius Scribonius Largus penned his *Prescriptions* around AD 47.
The English translation used here is one provided by Michael Hendry
in his blog post "Ancient Shock Therapy?" *Curculio*, November 8,
2005 (https://curculio.org/?p=67).

Details of the history of goldfish rearing in Japan were found in
Anna Marie Roos, *Goldfish* (London: Reaktion Books, 2019).

Katsushika Hokusai's *Goldfish Vendor* may be consulted on the

Minneapolis Institute of Art's online collection, via the following reference details: Katsushika Hokusai (1760–1849), *Goldfish Vendor*, woodblock print (surimono); ink and colour on paper (7 5/16 x 20 1/16 in.), Minneapolis Institute of Art, 1800s. Bequest of Richard P. Gale. Item 74.1.324.

Speaking Reliquary

Information on "speaking" reliquaries comes from Columbia University's online art history resource Treasures of Heaven. Regarding the Coogee shark arm case, I owe thanks to the online Dictionary of Sydney.

What Manner of Land

Information on Nibilio Gaggini and Pietro Rizzo's silver simulacrum of Santa Lucia (d. 1599) appears in Giovanni di Raimondo's article "Il Simulacro argenteo di Santa Lucia: Quattro secoli di storia" in *I Siracusani: Bimestrale di arte e tradizioni*, anno V, no. 26, July/August 2000.

My thanks to the BBC's religion resource centre for details of Saint Lucy's hagiography, posted on July 31, 2009 (https://www.bbc .co.uk/religion/religions/christianity/saints/lucy.shtml).

Likewise, I wish to thank Colin Dickey for his insightful and enjoyable article about Saint Lucy's life, works, and significance: "The Patron Saint of Dark Days: Vincent Van Gogh, Meet Saint Lucy," *Lapham's Quarterly*, December 22, 2011.

For their accounts of Italy's Santa Lucia celebrations, I am grateful to Slow Italy's travel segment "Santa Lucia Celebration in Italy" (http://slowitaly.yourguidetoitaly.com/santa-lucia-celebration-in -italy/), and Kayla Plantano's "Happy Saint Lucy's Day in Italy," published on i-Italy, December 2, 2018 (http://www.iitaly.org/magazine /focus/life-people/article/happy-saint-lucys-day-in-italy).

The painting referenced is Francesco del Cossa's *Saint Lucy*, c. 1473/1474, tempera on poplar panel, housed in the National Gallery of Art, Washington, D.C.

The full reference for the quotation from *The Epic of Gilgamesh* reads: *The Epic of Gilgamesh*, trans. N. K. Sandars (London: Penguin Books, 1962).

A series of articles in *Dezeen* magazine provided intriguing information on the world's "blackest blacks," Vantablack, and Anish Kapoor's purchase of its rights, as well as Stuart Semple's Black 3.0. These include Alice Morby's "Anish Kapoor Receives Exclusive Rights to Blackest Black in the World," March 2, 2016 (https://www.dezeen.com/2016/03/02/anish-kapoor-exclusive -rights-vantablack-blackest-black-pigment/); Gunseli Yalcinkaya's "Black 3.0 Is a 'Black Hole in a Bottle' That Challenges Anish Kapoor's Vantablack Pigment," February 5, 2019 (https://www .dezeen.com/2019/02/05/black-3-0-stuart-semple-anish-kapoor -vantablack/); and India Block's "MIT Creates Blackest Black That Is Darker Than Vantablack," September 24, 2019 (https://www.dezeen .com/2019/09/24/blackest-black-mit-material-news-vantablack/).

The full reference for the quotation from *The Egyptian Book of the Dead* is as follows: "CLXXV: The Chapter of Not Dying a Second Time" in *The Egyptian Book of the Dead: The Papyrus of Ani (Book of Coming Forth Today from Night: REU M PERT M HRU EN KHER)*, trans. E. A. Wallis Budge (Brooklyn: A&B Publishers Group [1894], 1999), p. 342.

The full reference for the passage from Ovid is "The House of Sleep, XI," *Metamorphoses*, AD 8, trans. A. S. Kline (Ann Arbor: Borders Classics, 2004).

The full citation record for Derek Jarman's *Chroma* is "Black Arts: O Mia Anima Nera," *Chroma—A Book of Colour—June '93* (London: Vintage, 1994).

Note that the quotation from Heinrich Zimmer's *Maya: Der indische Mythos* (Munich: Deutsche Verlag-Anstalt, 1936) first came to my attention when it was quoted in C. G. Jung's *Children's Dreams: Notes from the Seminar Given in 1936–1940* (Princeton: Princeton University Press, 2010). I cannot, however, find the quotation in the official English translation of Zimmer's work.

Kassia St. Clair's *The Secret Lives of Colour* (London: John Murray, 2016) was an invaluable resource when researching the his- tory of all manner of pigments in connection with this essay.

With the Moths' Eyes

Carolus Linnaeus, *Systema naturae 1735: Facsimile of the First Edition with an Introduction and a First English Translation of the "Observationes,"* eds. M. S. J. Engel-Ledeboer and H. Engel (Nieuwkoop, Netherlands: B. de Graaf, 1964), p. 19.

The section beginning "On the bedside table" takes its inspiration from Krzysztof Kieślowski's short documentary *Szpital / Hospital* and Andrei Tarkovsky's *Zerkalo / Mirror*.

Georgia Petridou's translation of Iamblichus's *Theurgia* is taken from Petridou's *Divine Epiphany in Greek Literature and Culture* (Oxford: Oxford University Press, 2015).

Information on Schumann resonance is based upon Miroslaw Kozlowski and Janina Marciak-Kozlowska's article "Schumann Resonance and Brain Waves: A Quantum Description," *Neuroquantology*, vol. 13, no. 2, 2015.

The full reference for *The Yellow Emperor's Classic of Internal Medicine* is as follows: *Huang Ti Nei Ching Su Wen, The Yellow Emperor's Classic of Internal Medicine*, trans. Ilza Veith (Berkeley: University of California Press, 2015).

The section commencing "A man notes his heart rate and dates it" is informed by Colin J. Pennycuik's research paper "Wingbeat Frequency of Birds in Steady Cruising Flight: New Data and Improved Predictions," *Journal of Experimental Biology*, vol. 199, issue 7, 1996, pp. 1613–1618; and Julian Simmons's photograph *Sarah Lucas with Dove*.

The full reference for Hippocrates' *Aphorisms* is as follows: Hippocrates, *Nature of Man. Regimen in Health. Humours. Aphorisms. Regimen 1–3. Dreams. Heracleitus: On the Universe*, trans. W. H. S. Jones (Cambridge: Loeb Classical Library, Harvard University Press, 1931).

The section beginning "A bathroom: rosy pink, glazed ceramic" draws visually from Sarah Lucas's photograph *Got a Salmon on #3* and Barry Jenkins's film *Moonlight*.

The citation of Qenherkhopshef the Younger appears in Philippa Lang, *Medicine and Society in Ptolemaic Egypt* (Leiden, Netherlands, and Boston: Brill Publishers, 2013), p. 52.

The section "Shopfront. Blue neon: *TVS USED & NEW* hovers beside a bulb killing flies" borrows from the imagery of Andrei Tarkovsky's *Stalker*.

As indicated in the text, the cure for red murrain is taken from *German-Russian Folk Medicine*, c. 1856–1942, trans. Dale Lee Wahl. These papers are held in the Calgary Chapter's library of the American Historical Society of Germans from Russia (chartered June 1987).

Last Night, the Sea Spat My Body

I am grateful to several scholars for their research on Jeanne Villepreux-Power, all of which greatly aided the passages appearing in this essay. Sources included the following:

Richard Owen's "Mollusca" appears as an entry in *Encyclopaedia Britannica*, Eighth Edition, vol. XV, 1858, p. 328. This was, in turn, brought to my attention by the works of Claude Arnal—a central scholar of Jeanne Villepreux-Power who provided many hours of enjoyable reading.

Claude Arnal's "La dame des Argonautes," *Bulletin des lettres, sciences et arts de la Corrèze*, 1994, pp. 179–189.

Claude Arnal's "Jeannette Villepreux Power à Messine: l'Argonauta argo et l'invention de l'aquarium (1832)." Written for the Congrès de Messine and read by Michela d'Angelo, 2010.

Marissa Fessenden's "A 19th Century Shipwreck Might Be Why This Famous Female Naturalist Faded to Obscurity," *Smithsonian Magazine*, June 2, 2015.

Ink

Aëtius's mention of an ancient tattoo ink originally appears in the Latin volume *Artis medicae principes, Hippocrates, Aretaeus, Alexander, Aurelianus, Celsus, Rhazeus* (Lausanne, Switzerland: sumptibus Franc. Grasset & Socior, 1772). This, in turn, was brought to my attention thanks to Vince Hemingson's *Tattoo Design Directory: The Essential Reference for Body Art* (London: A&C Black, 2008).

I found the anecdote of Wilhelm Joest's tattoo in Japan in W. R. Van Gulik, *Irezumi: The Pattern of Dermatography in Japan* (Rijksmuseum voor Volkenkunde, Leiden, Netherlands: E. J. Brill, 1982).

Anything That Makes a Mark, Anything That Takes a Mark

Vince Hemingson's *Tattoo Design Directory: The Essential Reference for Body Art* (London: A&C Black, 2008) proved an extensive resource for this essay. Information on varying tattoo traditions, notably the Maori styles mentioned, were sourced from this book.

I wish to thank W. R. Van Gulik for his research into the history of Japanese tattooing, which proved invaluable. Thus, references to Japanese histories of tattooing first appear in W. R. Van Gulik, *Irezumi: The Pattern of Dermatography in Japan* (Rijksmuseum voor Volkenkunde, Leiden, Netherlands: E. J. Brill, 1982).

Song Dong's *Stamping the Water* exists in photographic form, for which the full reference is as follows: *Stamping the Water* (performance in the Lhasa River, Tibet, 1996). Set of thirty-six chromogenic prints signed in Chinese, dated 1996, and released in a limited series of twelve print runs. Dimensions: 61 x 40 cm.; 24 x 15.7 in. (each).

The anecdotes of tattooing and branding in antiquity are to be found in the illuminating work of C. P. Jones, "Stigma: Tattooing and Branding in Graeco-Roman Antiquity," *Journal of Roman Studies*, vol. 77, 1987, pp. 139–155 (www.jstor.org/stable/300578, accessed January 27, 2020).

Direct quotations of Herodotus are taken from the following translation: Herodotus, *The Histories* with an English translation by A. D. Godley (Cambridge: Harvard University Press, 1920), book 7, section 35.

Information pertaining to the oldest tattoos on record was sourced from the Hermitage Museum's website in an article titled "The Hermitage News: Discovery of Tattoos on Ancient Mummies from Siberia," February 15, 2005.

Thanks to Lydia Pyne for her article "A History of Ink in Six Objects" that elucidated the history of indelible and iron gall ink, published on *History Today*, May 16, 2018 (https://www.historytoday .com/history-matters/history-ink-six-objects).

Zhang Huan's comment on the body as language is cited from an interview with RoseLee Goldberg featured in *Zhang Huan* (London and New York: Phaidon, 2009).

Likewise, I am grateful to several resources for their detailed accounts and critical research into the art of Zhang Huan. These include the following.

Wu Hung's "Speaking the Unspeakable" for its evocation of *12 Square Meters*, and, particularly, in its publication of a letter from Kong Ring—Zhang Huan's photographer for the work—featured in *Transience, Chinese Experimental Art at the End of the Twentieth Century* (Chicago: Smart Art Museum, 1999).

Kong Bu's essay "Zhang Huan in Beijing" for its detailed description of the work *65 Kilograms*, in the volume Melissa Chiu, Kong Bu, and Eleanor Heartney (authors), Zhang Huan (artist), *Zhang Huan: Altered States* (New York: Asia Society, 2007).

Winston Kyan's "The Buddhist Resistance of Zhang Huan's *Pagoda*" for its interrogation of *Pilgrimage—Wind and Water in*

New York, 1998. Published in *Art Journal Open* (a publication of the College Art Association of America), October 16, 2018 (http://artjournal.collegeart.org/?p=10012).

Likewise, my thanks to the Artspace editorial piece "'New York Made Me Sick at Heart': Performance Artist Zhang Huan Reflects on How America Made Him More Chinese," October 13, 2017 (https://www.artspace.com/magazine/interviews_features/book_report/new_york_made_me_sick_at_heart_zhang_huan-55042).

Quoted descriptions of Zhang Huan's *Family Tree* are taken from the Metropolitan Museum of Art's online collection description (https://www.metmuseum.org/art/collection/search/631073) and the Phillips auction house catalogue for its sale of Zhang Huan's "Family Tree," 2001: Nine chromogenic prints; dimensions 49 1/2 x 39 in. / 125.7 x 99.1 cm. (each); AP 2/2 from an edition of 8 plus 2 artist's proofs. Sale led by Caroline Deck, senior specialist, alongside Vanessa Hallett, worldwide head of photographs and deputy chairman, Americas (https://www.phillips.com/detail/zhang-huan/NY040017/18).

For Jean de Thévenot's description of pilgrim tattoos in seventeenth-century Jerusalem: Jean de Thévenot, *The Travels of Monsieur de Thévenot into the Levant in Three Parts, viz. into I. Turkey, II. Persia, III. the East-Indies, 1633–1667* (London: Printed by H. Clark, for H. Faithorne, J. Adamson, C. Skegnes, and T. Newborough, 1687).

Medicinal recipes from *The Papyrus Ebers* appear in *The Papyrus Ebers*, trans. from the German by Cyril P. Bryan with an introduction by G. Elliot Smith (Chicago: Ares Publishing, 1930).

The full reference for Stephen King's book on craft is as follows: Stephen King, *On Writing: A Memoir of the Craft* (New York: Scribner, 2000).

References to Cai Guo-Qiang's works occur in the film *Sky Ladder: The Art of Cai Guo-Qiang*, director Kevin Macdonald, music composed by Alex Heffes, producers Wendi Murdoch, Hugo Shong, and Fisher Stevens, cinematography by Robert Yeoman and Florian Zinke, October 14, 2016.

The full reference for Melati Suryodarmo's work is: Melati Suryodarmo (b. 1969), *Eins und Eins (One and One)*: Basin, paper, imitation ink (water, food colouring), black garments, white shoes. Two-hour performance, Pearl Lam Galleries, Singapore, 2016.

The full reference for quoted material from Pierre Bayard is as follows: Pierre Bayard, *How to Talk about Books You Haven't Read*, trans. Jeffrey Mehlman (London: Granta Books, 2008). Note that I rearranged the sequencing of the quoted material for aesthetic effect. Thus, the last line quoted—"Our relation to books is a shadowy space haunted by the ghosts of memory, and the real value of books lies in their ability to conjure these specters"—actually appears in the preface, long before the section on forgotten books.

For Maurice Merleau-Ponty's unfinished last work: Maurice Merleau-Ponty, *Le visible et l'invisible* (Paris: Éditions Gallimard, 1964); and, in English, Maurice Merleau-Ponty, *The Visible and the Invisible*, trans. Alphonso Lingis (Evanston: Northwestern University Press, 1968).

And the Lord Spake unto the Fish

Information on the eating habits of sharks and whales was compiled from the following articles: Holly Richmond, "Your Plastic Garbage Is Killing Whales," *Grist*, November 11, 2013; Grace Constantino, "Sharks Were Once Called Sea Dogs, and Other Little-Known Facts," Biodiversity Heritage Library, August 12, 2014; Anonymous, "Bizarre: 11 Weirdest Things Found inside Sharks' Stomachs," *Deccan Chronicle*, July 25, 2018; Michael Rogers, "The 14 Weirdest Things Sharks Have Eaten," *Sharksider*, August 8, 2016.

Last Night, the Moon Flooded the Bedclothes

The full reference for the quoted material from Claudius Aelian's *On the Nature of Animals* is as follows: "Divination by Fishes," Claudius Aelian (c. AD 175–c. 235), in *De natura animalium* or *On the Nature of Animals,* trans. A. F. Scholfield (Cambridge: Harvard University Press, 1958), VIII.V.

. An extensive account of the Pennsylvania fisheries exhibit at the St. Louis World's Fair is contained in James H. Lambert, executive officer Pennsylvania Commission, *The Story of Pennsylvania at the World's Fair St. Louis, 1904, vol. 2* (Philadelphia: Pennsylvania Commission, 1905).

The full reference for the quotation from Plutarch reads: "Why the Pythagoreans Command Fish Not to Be Eaten, More Strictly Than Other Animals" in *Quaestiones convivales* compiled within *Plutarch's Morals.* Translated from the Greek by several hands. Corrected and revised by William W. Goodwin (Boston: Little, Brown, and Cambridge: Press of John Wilson and son, 1874), vol. 8, chap. 8, section 3.

Information on Leonhardt Thurneysser first appeared in several sources. The earliest recorded mention of the birdcage within a fishbowl comes in Johann Karl Wilhelm Moehsen's *Beiträge zur Geschichte der Wissenschaften in der Mark Brandenburg von den ältesten Zeiten an bis zu Ende des sechszehnten Jahrhunderts* [Contributions to the history of science in the Mark Brandenburg from the earliest times to the end of the sixteenth century] (Berlin and Leipzig, Germany: Decker, 1783) (available online at http://mdz -nbn-resolving.de/urn:nbn:de:bvb:12-bsbl0711246-6).

A second, later mention is made in Jakob Wassermann's *Deutsche charaktere und begebenheiten* [German characters and events] (Berlin: S. Fischer, 1915) (available online at http://www.gutenberg.org/files /18258/18258-8.txt).

There seems to be some conflict between sources over whether the bird in Thurneysser's creation was, in fact, live or blown from glass. Nonetheless, the later birdcage-fishbowl creations of the 1825–1840 period most definitely housed live fish and live birds. For further information on these rarely studied aquariums, consult Helmut Ricke's "Der Vogel Im Goldfischglas," *Journal of Glass Studies,* vol. 59, 2017, pp. 261–284.

The allegation that Thurneysser invented swathes of text in his works appears in James Campbell Brown (1843–1910), *A History of Chemistry from the Earliest Times by the Late James Campbell Brown* (London: J. & A. Churchill, 1920). Brown writes: "He was accused more appropriately of having a devil in a bottle which taught him to write in languages of which he was ignorant, a very convenient familiar, especially if we are to believe Bollenhagen, who asserted that Thurneysser's knowledge of languages was lamentably deficient."

As for Thurneysser's stained-glass window cycle, Isobel Leybold-Johnson wrote an insightful article when Basel's Kunstmuseum exhibited two of the remaining windows in 2010–2011. See Isobel Leybold-Johnson, "Basel's 16th-Century Superstar," *Swissinfo*, November 24, 2010 (https://www.swissinfo.ch/eng/basel-s-16th -century-superstar/28863378).

Tongue Stones

The quotation from Pliny the Elder is taken from his *Naturalis historia*, trans. John Bostock, M.D., F.R.S. H. T. Riley, Esq., B.A. (London: Taylor and Francis, Red Lion Court, Fleet Street, 1855), vol. 37, chap. 59.

For information pertaining to the use of "tongue stones" as medicinal amulets, I am indebted to the Pitt Rivers Museum's online collection *Small Blessings: Amulets at the Pitt Rivers Museum.* Transferred from the Wellcome Institute in 1985, the exhibit *Tongue Stone, France*, inventory number 1985.52.774, can be viewed online (http://web.prm.ox.ac.uk/amulets/index.php/tooth-amulet5 /index.html).

G. Zammit Maempel's article "Handbills Extolling the Virtues of Fossil Shark's Teeth" also proved invaluable in its research of Maltese history and myths, published in *Melita Historica: A Journal of Maltese History*, vol. 7, no. 3 (1978): pp. 211–224, and available online.

Information regarding the great white shark caught off the Livorno coast first appeared in Alessandro De Maddalena and Walter Heim's *Mediterranean Great White Sharks: A Comprehensive Study Including All Recorded Sightings* (London: McFarland, 2012), p. 42.

Likewise, I owe thanks to R. Aidan Martin's article "*Glossopetrae* and the Birth of Paleontology," published on the ReefQuest Centre for Shark Research website (http://www.elasmo-research.org/education /evolution/glossopetrae.htm), which provided a detailed account of the dissection and its scientific ramifications.

I Am Poured Out Like Water

Many thanks to Jeannette Doval and Jaquira Díaz for talking to me of la Noche de San Juan and answering my numerous questions. Details concerning the Puerto Rican tradition of la Noche de San Juan in New York were found in Robin Shulman's article "A Watery Ritual to Erase Bad Luck and Reverse It," *New York Times*, June 25, 2005 (https://www.nytimes.com/2005/06/25/nyregion/a-watery -ritual-to-erase-bad-luck-and-reverse-it.html).

Statistics concerning the body's survival times in cold water come from Kevin Monahan's *Local Knowledge: A Skipper's Reference* (Qualicum Beach, BC, Canada: Fine Edge: Nautical & Recreational Publishing, 2005).

The full reference for the citation of Gaston Bachelard is as follows: Gaston Bachelard, *Water and Dreams: An Essay on the Imagination of Matter*, trans. E. R. Farrell (Dallas: Pegasus Foundation, 1983).

When researching information on the decline of the Dead Sea, Joshua Hammer's article "The Dying of the Dead Sea," *Smithsonian Magazine*, October 2005 (https://www.smithsonianmag.com/science -nature/the-dying-of-the-dead-sea-70079351/), proved a great help.

Excerpts from the works of seventeenth-century French explorer Jean de Thévenot are quoted from "*Chapter XLI. Of the River of Jordan*, of the Dead-Sea, and of the Mount of the Forty Days Fast" in Jean de Thévenot, *The Travels of Monsieur de Thévenot into the Levant in Three Parts, viz. into I. Turkey, II. Persia, III. the East-*

Indies, 1633–1667 (London: Printed by H. Clark, for H. Faithorne, J. Adamson, C. Skegnes, and T. Newborough, 1687).

Facts related to the aquatic composition of the human body are quoted from H. H. Mitchell, T. S. Hamilton, F. R. Steggerda, and H. W. Bean, "The Chemical Composition of the Adult Human Body and Its Bearing on the Biochemistry of Growth," *Journal of Biological Chemistry*, vol. 158, 1945, pp. 625–637.

For details of the Dead Sea swim, I am indebted to Uri Talshir's article "Swimmers Cross Dead Sea for First Time, Carefully," *Haaretz*, November 16, 2006 (https://www.haaretz.com/israel-news/.premium.MAGAZINE-swimmers-cross-dead-sea-for-first-time-carefully-1.5462239), and the article "Swimmers Prove Their Salt in 7-Hour Crawl across Shrinking Dead Sea," *Times of Israel*, November 16, 2006 (https://www.timesofisrael.com/swimmers-prove-their-salt-in-7-hour-crawl-across-shrinking-dead-sea/).

The Dead Sea scroll: *"A Baptismal Liturgy," 4Q414, F.12*, is quoted from the Gnostic Society Library (http://www.gnosis.org/library/baptl.htm).

As concerns details of the Dead Sea scroll forgeries, I am grateful to the in-depth research of Michael Greshko's article "'Dead Sea Scrolls' at the Museum of the Bible Are All Forgeries," *National Geographic*, March 17, 2020 (https://www.nationalgeographic.co.uk/history-and-civilisation/2020/03/dead-sea-scrolls-museum-of-bible-are-all-forgeries).

The full reference for Mircea Eliade's work is as follows: Mircea Eliade, *Patterns in Comparative Religion*, trans. Rosemary Sheed (Lincoln and London: University of Nebraska Press, 1996), pp. 194–195.

Last Night, Eels Crashed from the Faucet

The full reference for Pliny the Elder's hypothesis on eel reproduction is: Pliny the Elder, *Naturalis historia* [IX:LXXIV], trans. H. Rackham (vols. 1–5, 9), W. H. S. Jones (vols. 6–8), and D. E.

Eichholz (vol. 10) (Cambridge: Loeb Classical Library, Harvard University Press, 1940).

Information pertaining to the recovery of ancient Egyptian votive boxes, particularly those depicting and containing mummified eels, originally appears in W. M. F. Petrie, *Naukratis. Part I, 1884–5*, Third Memoir of the Egypt Exploration Fund (London: Trübner and Co. 1886), pp. 41–42.

Examples of eel votive boxes may be consulted in the British Museum's collection. One such item includes *Votive box; figure*, 500 BC–350 BC [acquired 1885]. Excavated by Egypt Exploration Fund. Excavated at: Naukratis, Nile Delta, Egypt. Copper alloy. Museum number BM: EA27581, registration number: 1885,1101.81.

Thanks also to Patrik Svensson for his illuminating work *The Book of Eels: Our Enduring Fascination with the Most Mysterious Creature in the Natural World*, trans. Agnes Broomé (New York: Harper Collins, 2020); and to Jarvis Brooke for his review of Svensson's memoir in "Where Do Eels Come From?" *New Yorker*, May 25, 2020 (originally published in the May 25, 2020, print issue under the title "Slippery Truth," and subsequently posted online). Both of these sources provided insightful information on the morphology and lifespan of the European eel.

The full references for quoted material from Aelian's *On the Nature of Animals* are as follows:

Claudius Aelian (c. AD 175–c. 235), "The Moray and the Viper," in *De natura animalium* or *On the Nature of Animals*, trans. A. F. Scholfield (Cambridge: Harvard University Press, 1958), I:L.

Claudius Aelian (c. AD 175–c. 235), "The Depths of the Sea," in *De natura animalium* or *On the Nature of Animals*, trans. A. F. Scholfield (Cambridge: Harvard University Press, 1958), IX:XXXV.

Additional Works Consulted

Although the following works are not directly referenced, they animated and informed my thinking during this project. I wish to thank their authors and include a list here.

Rebecca Stott, *Theatres of Glass: The Woman Who Brought the Sea to the City* (London: Short Books, 2003).

For information on the early and ongoing practices of aquarium collection: Samantha Muka's insightful article "Bursting the Aquarium Bubble," *Atlantic*, April 25, 2019; Justin McCurry's "'Sick to My Stomach': Dolphin and Penguins Locked in Derelict Japan Aquarium," *Guardian*, August 31, 2018; and Mark J. Palmer's "Honey the Dolphin Dies Alone in Japan Park" on the International Marine Mammal Project (IMMP) website, April 16, 2020.

Thanks likewise to Sarah Zhang for her fascinating article on aquarium water quality and management: "How a Landlocked Aquarium Gets Its Seawater," *Atlantic*, November 8, 2018.

Permission Acknowledgments

Acknowledgments

I am indebted to Graywolf Press for believing in this manuscript. I owe particular thanks to my editor, Steve Woodward, whose insightful reading, incisive fine-tuning, and endurance of my Briticisms transformed this manuscript into its best self.

For your time, effort, and hard work, thank you, also, to Chantz Erolin, Katie Dublinski, Marisa Atkinson, Caroline Nitz, Claudia Acevedo-Quiñones, Casey O'Neil, Ill Nippashi, Morgan LaRocca, Shaina Robinson, and everyone at Graywolf who brought this book into being.

I am grateful to my agent, PJ Mark, for his kindness, enthusiasm, and invaluable reading of the work.

My sincere thanks to Natalie Diaz for generously permitting "The First Water Is the Body" to be quoted as an epigraph to this book.

Maaza Mengiste, your support, encouragement, and kindness are a light. Thank you.

Jenny Xu, thank you for reading this manuscript in its earliest stages. What razor-sharp insight. And generous encouragement.

During the writing of this book, the Sewanee Writers' Conference provided me with a nonfiction fellowship, the *Kenyon Review* published early versions of "In Water Disjointed from Me" and "With the Moths' Eyes," and the *Virginia Quarterly Review* published "The Georgian Military Road." Each gesture aided and revitalised the project.

To all the creative writing faculty at Concordia University, Montreal, and to those professors with whom I took classes at McGill University, Montreal: Thank you. Even if this manuscript came after my time with you, your instruction and guidance have remained with me. Lifelong tools, rich gifts.

For all the ways you have carried me, thank you to my family and friends. I would never have made it, nor written this book, without your love, loyalty, and encouragement.

And Jaqui, my water away from water, my beginning and ending— bright, magic, vital. That the world lets me live in this, in baptism, in a blessing.

LARS HORN is a writer and translator working in literary and experimental nonfiction. The recipient of a Sewanee Writers' Conference scholarship, Horn has written for the *Virginia Quarterly Review*, the *Kenyon Review*, and elsewhere. Initially specialising in phenomenology and visual arts scholarship, they hold MAs from the University of Edinburgh, the École normale supérieure, Paris, and Concordia University, Montreal. They live in Miami with their wife, the writer Jaquira Díaz.

The Graywolf Press Nonfiction Prize

Voice of the Fish by Lars Horn is the 2020 winner of the Graywolf Press Nonfiction Prize. Graywolf awards this prize to a previously unpublished, full-length work of outstanding literary nonfiction by a writer who is not yet established in the genre.

The Graywolf Press Nonfiction Prize seeks to acknowledge—and honor—the great traditions of literary nonfiction. Whether grounded in observation, autobiography, or research, much of the most beautiful, daring, and original writing over the past few decades can be categorized as nonfiction.

Previous winners include *Names for Light: A Family History* by Thirii Myo Kyaw Myint, *The Collected Schizophrenias* by Esmé Weijun Wang, *Riverine: A Memoir from Anywhere but Here* by Angela Palm, *Leaving Orbit: Notes from the Last Days of American Spaceflight* by Margaret Lazarus Dean, *The Empathy Exams: Essays* by Leslie Jamison, *The Grey Album: On the Blackness of Blackness* by Kevin Young, *Notes from No Man's Land: American Essays* by Eula Biss, *Black Glasses Like Clark Kent: A GI's Secret from Postwar Japan* by Terese Svoboda, *Neck Deep and Other Predicaments* by Ander Monson, and *Frantic Transmissions to and from Los Angeles: An Accidental Memoir* by Kate Braverman.

The Graywolf Press Nonfiction Prize is funded in part by endowed gifts from the Arsham Ohanessian Charitable Remainder Unitrust and the Ruth Easton Fund of the Edelstein Family Foundation.

Arsham Ohanessian, an Armenian born in Iraq who came to the United States in 1952, was an avid reader and a tireless advocate for human rights and peace. He strongly believed in the power of literature and education to make a positive impact on humanity.

Ruth Easton, born in North Branch, Minnesota, was a Broadway actress in the 1920s and 1930s. The Ruth Easton Fund of the Edelstein Family Foundation is pleased to support the work of emerging artists and writers in her honor.

Graywolf Press is grateful to Arsham Ohanessian and Ruth Easton for their generous support.

The text of *Voice of the Fish* is set in Ehrhardt MT Pro.
Book design by Rachel Holscher.
Composition by Bookmobile Design and Digital
Publisher Services, Minneapolis, Minnesota.
Manufactured by McNaughton & Gunn on acid-free,
100 percent postconsumer wastepaper.